¡Ven conmigo!

Holt Spanish
Level 3

Grammar and Vocabulary
Reteaching and Practice
Workbook

HOLT, RINEHART AND WINSTON
Harcourt Brace & Company
Austin • New York • Orlando • Atlanta • San Francisco • Boston • Dallas • Toronto • London

Requests for permission to make copies of any part of the work should be mailed to: Permissions Department, Holt, Rinehart and Winston, Inc., 6277 Sea Harbor Drive, Orlando, Florida 32887-6777.

¡VEN CONMIGO! is a registered trademark licensed to Holt, Rinehart and Winston.

Printed in the United States of America

ISBN 0-03-051383-9

2   3   4   5   6   7   8   9   021   00   99   98   97

Contents

CAPÍTULO 1 ¡Qué bien lo pasé este verano!

■ PRIMER PASO

To express interest, indifference, and displeasure toward activities, you'll need to know vocabulary for hobbies. You'll also need to use the present and preterite tenses.

VOCABULARIO   Deportes y pasatiempos   *Pupil's Edition, p. 10*

1 Fill in the following blanks with the correct word from the word box to find out what Flori and her friends like and don't like to do.

| bucear | el clarinete | las cartas | montañismo | sellos |
| las revistas | la equitación | patinar | la fotografía |

1. Me fascina la historia del correo, por eso me la paso coleccionando _____.

2. Martín está loco por _____. Monta todos los días a su caballo Pudín.

3. A Sara le parece un rollo jugar a _____.

4. Yo, en cambio, estoy loca por la música. Toco _____ y me encanta.

5. Una fanática del _____ es Kika. Se la pasa escalando montañas.

6. A Gisela no le gusta para nada _____. Nunca quiere sacar fotos.

2 You're planning activities for a weekend retreat. Based on the following popularity rankings, place a check mark next to the facilities and equipment you want to reserve.

patinaje	videojuegos	cartas	remo	esquí acuático	ciclismo	música	playa
11%	25%	3%	1%	5%	17%	19%	19%

_____ music room   _____ photo lab

_____ diving equipment   _____ video arcade

_____ reading room   _____ mountain-climbing equipment

_____ skating rink   _____ water skis

_____ picnic area on the beach   _____ bicycles

_____ rowing equipment   _____ recreation room

*G*ramática de repaso Present tense of stem-changing verbs *Pupil's Edition, p. 11*

Some verbs have a stem change in the present tense in all forms except the **nosotros** and **vosotros** forms. The following are the three types of stem changes:

  e → ie (empezar: emp**ie**zo, emp**ie**zas, emp**ie**za, emp**e**zamos, emp**e**záis, emp**ie**zan)

  o → ue (contar: c**ue**nto, c**ue**ntas, c**ue**nta, c**o**ntamos, c**o**ntáis, c**ue**ntan)

  e → i (servir: s**i**rvo, s**i**rves, s**i**rve, s**e**rvimos, s**e**rvís, s**i**rven)

3 Conjugate the following stem-changing verbs in the present tense .

  1. pedir _____

  2. sentir _____

  3. preferir _____

  4. dormir _____

  5. empezar _____

  6. contar _____

  7. servir _____

  8. querer _____

4 Yoli can't decide whether to go to the orchestra concert tonight. Fill in the following blanks with the correct present-tense form of the verb in parentheses.

  MARI Oye, Yoli, el concierto estudiantil **(1)** _____ (empezar) en veinte minutos.

     Juan y yo vamos a ir. ¿Tú **(2)** _____ (querer) ir con nosotros?

  YOLI No sé. ¿Quién más va a ir?

  MARI Mi hermana no va. No le gustan los conciertos. Ella **(3)** _____ (preferir)

     escuchar música por la radio. Tampoco **(4)** _____ (poder) ir Clara y Julio.

     Es que ellos **(5)** _____ (tener) que trabajar esta noche.

  YOLI ¿Va a ser buena la música?

  MARI Claro que sí. Siempre es muy buena. Por eso Juan y yo siempre nos **(6)** _____

     (sentar) muy cerca de la orquesta. Y además, nosotros **(7)** _____ (pensar)
     que es un buen día para un concierto.

  YOLI Todavía no sé. Dicen que los conciertos son aburridos y que muchos estudiantes

     (8) _____ (dormir) durante la música.

  MARI Es posible, pero hay una recepción que **(9)** _____ (seguir) el concierto

     y los estudiantes **(10)** _____ (servir) refrescos. Eso sí te va a gustar.

5 While at the recreation center this weekend, you saw the following list of rules. Fill in the blanks with the correct form of the present tense of the verbs in parentheses.

Reglamentos del parque

1. El parque _____ (cerrar) a las diez de la noche.

2. Los dependientes del parque _____ (servir) refrescos en el patio.

3. Los niños menores de 10 años no _____ (poder) nadar en el lago.

4. La policía _____ (empezar) a pasar por el área a las nueve.

5. Los salvavidas no _____ (venir) hasta las nueve.

6. Si Ud. _____ (querer) bucear, _____ (tener) que usar el equipo apropiado.

7. Tengan cuidado al pasar por el parque cuando los niños _____ (jugar) en el césped.

8. Si Ud. _____ (preferir) hacer un picnic cerca del lago, es necesario hablar con la gerencia.

¿Se te ha olvidado?   The present tense   *Pupil's Edition, p. 336-356*

6 Write a letter to a pen pal by forming sentences from these notes.

1. Mi familia y yo / vivir en Valparaíso

_____

_____

2. Mi hermano Carlos y su amigo / practicar el tenis

_____

_____

3. Sandra / ir a la playa los fines de semana

_____

_____

4. Pablo / estudiar en la biblioteca

_____

_____

5. Mis amigos / comer en el café Pueblito

_____

_____

*G*ramática de repaso   The preterite tense   *Pupil's Edition, p. 12*

- The preterite tense of regular verbs is formed by dropping the -**ar**, -**er**, or -**ir** of the infinitive and adding the preterite endings. Verbs that end in -**er** and -**ir** have the same endings in the preterite.

montar (-ar)		comer (-er/-ir)	
yo mont**é**	nosotros mont**amos**	yo com**í**	nosotros com**imos**
tú mont**aste**	vosotros mont**asteis**	tú com**iste**	vosotros com**isteis**
él/ella/Ud. mont**ó**	ellos/ellas/Uds. mont**aron**	él/ella/Ud. com**ió**	ellos/ellas/Uds. com**ieron**

- In the first person plural for -**ar** and -**ir** verbs, the forms of the present and preterite are the same. The context will make the meaning clear:

    Ayer remamos en el lago y hoy remamos en el río.

7 Change the verbs in parentheses in the following sentences to their corresponding forms in the preterite tense.

1. Juan _____ (pasear) en velero todo el verano.

2. ¿Tú _____ (leer) todas las revistas en la biblioteca?

3. Le _____ (gustar) mucho esta película.

4. Yo _____ (escalar) montañas en los Andes esta Navidad.

5. Juanita _____ (jugar) a las cartas durante el fin de semana.

6. David y Nena _____ (tocar) el clarinete en nuestros conciertos.

7. Juan y yo _____ (escuchar) música por muchas horas.

8. ¿ _____ (montar) tú mucho a caballo?

9. Hernán y yo _____ (leer) libros de ciencia ficción.

8 Complete each of the following sentences with the correct preterite form of the verb in parentheses.

1. Este verano nosotros lo _____ (pasar) muy bien en Bolivia.

2. Yo _____ (visitar) a mis primos en La Paz.

3. Ellos y yo _____ (hablar) de muchas cosas divertidas.

4. Nosotros _____ (patinar) en línea en la plaza.

5. También nosotros _____ (montar) a caballo por las montañas.

6. Yo _____ (bucear) en el Lago Titicaca.

7. Mi prima nos _____ (tocar) muchas canciones en el piano.

8. Durante mi visita yo _____ (tomar) muchas fotos.

9. ¿ _____ (remar) tú mucho en el lago?

9 Fill in the blanks in the following paragraph with the correct preterite form of the verb in parentheses to tell what you did last summer.

Este verano **(1)** _____ (ser) increíble para mí. Mi familia y yo

(2) _____ (ir) a España. Nosotros **(3)** _____

(visitar) a mis abuelos que viven en Murcia. Ellos viven cerca de la playa. Nosotros

(4) _____ (hacer) muchas cosas: **(5)** _____ (nadar)

y también, **(6)** _____ (bucear). Yo **(7)** _____

(pasear) en velero. Mi hermano **(8)** _____ (remar) todos los fines de

semana. Mis padres, en cambio, sólo **(9)** _____ (jugar) a las cartas con

mis abuelos. Mi primo, que también estuvo allí por el verano, **(10)** _____

(leer) mucho. Le encantan las tiras cómicas.

10 Write a logical completion for each of the following sentences to say what that person did or didn't do. Use the word **porque** plus the correct preterite form of the verb in parentheses.

MODELO   Tengo sueño . . . (dormir anoche)   **porque no dormí anoche.**

1. Juan está muy cansado . . . (patinar en línea tres horas)

   _____

2. Tienes mucha hambre . . . (comer esta mañana)

   _____

3. Ayanancy y Marta se sienten felices . . . (salir bien en el examen)

   _____

4. A Luisa y a mí nos duelen los oídos . . . (escuchar música fuerte)

   _____

5. Tengo mucha sed . . . (beber agua después de correr)

   _____

11 Write sentences telling what you and people you know did at the indicated times.

1. La semana pasada yo _____.

2. Anoche mi mejor amigo(a) _____.

3. Ayer mis amigos _____.

4. El fin de semana pasado mi familia _____.

5. Esta mañana mis compañeros de clase _____.

6. Ayer mis profesores _____.

■ SEGUNDO PASO

To ask for information, you'll need to know how to form questions. To describe yourself and others you'll need to know how to use adjectives.

 **ASÍ SE DICE**   Asking for information   *Pupil's Edition, p. 16*

12 Below is an excerpt of a transcript of a phone conversation Javier had with a company conducting an opinion poll. Fill in the blanks with the correct question word.

ENCUESTADOR   ¿ (1) _____ haces en tus ratos libres?
JAVIER   Bueno, me gusta mucho patinar en línea.

ENCUESTADOR   ¿Con (2) _____ lo haces? ¿Lo haces solo?
JAVIER   Muchas veces voy solo, pero de vez en cuando mis amigos me acompañan.

ENCUESTADOR   Muy bien. ¿ (3) _____ asistes a clases?
JAVIER   Este . . . las clases comienzan a las nueve y duran hasta las tres y media.

ENCUESTADOR   ¿ (4) _____ te gusta ir después de clases?
JAVIER   Después de clases me gusta ir a la biblioteca a estudiar.

ENCUESTADOR   ¿ (5) _____ vas allí?
JAVIER   Bueno, es necesario estudiar todos los días si quiero sacar buenas notas.

ENCUESTADOR   ¿ (6) _____ son tus clases?
JAVIER   A ver . . . Muchas son divertidas, pero no me gusta el arte.

13 Your Spanish Club is sending out a survey to students in Spanish-speaking countries. For each item, write a question that asks for the indicated information. Use the **tú** form.

1. name

   ¿ _____ ?

2. age

   ¿ _____ ?

3. where you like to go

   ¿ _____ ?

4. favorite free-time things to do

   ¿ _____ ?

5. times you have class

   ¿ _____ ?

6. favorite teacher

   ¿ _____ ?

VOCABULARIO   Para describir a la gente   *Pupil's Edition, p. 17*

14 For each set of words, write the word that doesn't belong with the others in the blank provided.

_____	1. simpático	fenomenal	aburrido	amable
_____	2. simpático	interesante	divertido	pesado
_____	3. abierto	buena gente	majo	antipático
_____	4. un gran tipo	no hay quien lo aguante	pesado	aburrido
_____	5. pesado	interesante	cómico	buena gente
_____	6. inteligente	listo	aplicado	no hay quien lo aguante
_____	7. bigote	barba	calvo	guapa
_____	8. gafas	serio	interesante	inteligente

15 Paraphrase the descriptions of the following people.

MODELO   Sara tiene el pelo rojo y mide 176 centímetros.   **Sara es pelirroja y alta.**

1. El Sr. Figueroa tiene pelo en la cara, pero no tiene pelo en la cabeza.

   _____

   _____

2. Marcos pasa mucho tiempo en la biblioteca. Sabe mucho de todas las materias. Saca las mejores notas de la clase.

   _____

   _____

3. Clara molesta mucho. Trata (*treats*) muy mal a todo el mundo; no tiene ningún amigo.

   _____

   _____

4. Maribel es mi mejor amiga. Siempre comparte (*shares*) todo conmigo.

   _____

   _____

5. Sebastián me cae muy bien. Es muy simpático.

   _____

   _____

6. Catalina es muy cómica; ¡nunca está seria!

   _____

   _____

*G*ramática de repaso   **saber** vs. **conocer**   *Pupil's Edition, p. 18*

Use **saber** to talk about knowing facts or to talk about knowing how to do something. Use **conocer** to talk about knowing a person, meeting a person, or being familiar with a place.

No sé si su hermano es amable pero **sabe** jugar muy bien al baloncesto.

Conozco muy bien a Isabel. Es muy amable.

16 Decide whether you would use **saber** or **conocer** to say that you know each of the following. Write the verb in the blanks to indicate your answer.

_____ 1. escalar montañas   _____ 5. una persona famosa

_____ 2. mi amiga Vivian   _____ 6. cuántos días hay en un año

_____ 3. la fecha de un día festivo   _____ 7. San Antonio, Texas

_____ 4. hablar alemán   _____ 8. tocar el piano

17 Fill in the blanks in Mariana's letter with the correct form of **saber** or **conocer**.

Tengo un problema. Mis padres me dicen que no puedo salir con Diego porque ellos no lo (1) _____. Creen que soy muy joven para él. Pero ellos ni siquiera (2) _____ cómo es. Yo lo (3) _____ desde hace mucho tiempo. También lo (4) _____ todas mis amigas y les cae muy bien. De todas maneras no (5) _____ si quiero salir con él. ¿(6) _____ Ud. qué debo hacer?

18 Fill in this conversation with Flori with the correct form of either **saber** or **conocer**.

CARLOS   Oye, Flori, ¿(1) _____ a alguien que tenga información sobre las universidades en España?

FLORI   No, pero (2) _____ un lugar donde ellos (3) _____ esa información.

CARLOS   ¿De veras? ¿Dónde está?

FLORI   No (4) _____ dónde está pero se llama El Centro Escolar.

CARLOS   ¿(Tú) (5) _____ si está abierto hoy?

FLORI   No, pero (6) _____ a alguien que trabaja allí. Se llama Minerva Ochoa.

CARLOS   No la (7) _____. ¿Puedes llamarla?

FLORI   Bueno, no (8) _____ si trabaja hoy, pero la puedo llamar.

Nota *G*ramatical   o → u and y → e   *Pupil's Edition, p. 18*

In Spanish, the word **o** *(or)* changes to **u** before words beginning with an "o" sound. The word **y** *(and)* changes to **e** before words beginning with an "i" sound. For example: María **e** Iván, Pedro **u** Olga

19 Make logical pairs by joining a word from the box on the left with a word from the box on the right with either **y** or **e**.

Fernando	guapo
hijos	María
español	Honorato

elegante	inglés
Inés	Isabel
hijas	Hilaria

1. _____   4. _____

2. _____   5. _____

3. _____   6. _____

20 Make logical choices by joining a word from the box on the left with a word from the box on the right with either **o** or **u**.

ayer	más
minutos	este
siete	mujeres

menos	ocho
horas	hoy
oeste	hombres

1. _____   4. _____

2. _____   5. _____

3. _____   6. _____

21 Cindy wrote the following note to her friend María José but left out the conjunctions **y** and **o**. Complete her note with **y** and **o**, changing them to **e** and **u** before certain sounds.

Hola, María José. ¿Qué tal? Tengo que decirte que ayer conocí a un chico muy guapo. Está en

mi clase de química. Es muy listo **(1)** _____ inteligente. Es de España. Mis amigos

(2) _____ yo queremos hacer una reunión para conocerlo mejor. El problema es

que no sabemos si la debemos hacer mañana **(3)** _____ hoy. No queremos esperar

pero hoy ya tengo planes para ir al centro comercial con Carlos **(4)** _____ Isabel.

Tampoco sabemos a cuántas personas invitar. Tal vez siete **(5)** _____ ocho. Tú,

¿qué piensas? Yo creo que basta con siete personas, más **(6)** _____ menos.

CAPÍTULO 2

Por una vida sana

■ PRIMER PASO

To ask for and give advice, you'll need to use informal commands. You'll also need to be familiar with expressions that people use to talk about their feelings and problems.

*G*ramática de repaso   Informal commands   *Pupil's Edition, p. 34*

The affirmative informal commands are the same as the **él/ella** form of the verb. Another way to think of forming them is by dropping the -**s** of the **tú** form of the verb.

> **Tú estudias. → ¡Estudia!**

The negative commands are formed by dropping the -**o** of the **yo** form and adding -**es** if it's an -**ar** verb and adding -**as** if it's an -**er** or an -**ir** verb.

> **Estudio. → ¡No estudies!   Salgo. → ¡No salgas!**

The following verbs have irregular affirmative commands:

poner → **pon**	ir → **ve (no vayas)**	tener → **ten**
venir → **ven**	decir → **di**	salir → **sal**

1 You need to tell your younger brother to do and not to do the following things. Write the informal commands of the following phrases.

1. ayudar a preparar el desayuno

   _____

2. beber el jugo

   _____

3. no despertar a papá

   _____

4. no correr en la casa

   _____

5. no comer pastel para el desayuno

   _____

6. lavar los platos

   _____

7. quitar la mesa

   _____

2 Follow each negative command with an affirmative command. Use the same verb.

1. No pongas la camisa allí. _____la en el armario.

2. No vengas a la reunión a las 7:30. _____ más temprano.

3. No salgas por esa puerta. _____ por ésta.

4. No digas mentiras. _____ siempre la verdad.

5. No vayas al cine solo. _____ con Laura.

6. No tengas miedo. ¡ _____ cuidado!

3 Give an appropriate piece of advice for each of the following situations using informal commands.

1. Estoy rendido. _____

2. Sufro de presiones. _____

3. Estoy aburrida. _____

4. Estoy histérica. _____

5. Me pongo nervioso durante un examen. _____

6. Estoy completamente agotado. _____

7. Estoy agobiada. _____

VOCABULARIO   El estrés   *Pupil's Edition, pp. 34–35*

4 Unscramble the following words.

<u>pista</u> (*clue*)	palabra revuelta
1. nerviosa	**anaioss**
2. loco	**ohiicrsté**
3. ser gracioso	**seeírr**
4. cansado	**gaadoot**
5. tranquilidad	**maacl**
6. tensiones	**neioprses**
7. cansadísima	**dadeinr**
8. debes	**ísdberae**

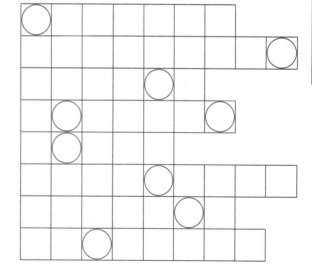

Now unscramble the circled letters to find out how Mauricio and his friends are feeling today.

_____

CAPÍTULO 2 Primer paso

5 Fill in Felipe's composition with an appropriate word from the box to find out what his family does about stress.

> presiones   cuida a tu hermano   queda   sufrimos   rendida
>
> tomar las cosas con calma   resolver   agotado   pone   agobiado
>
> cuidarse

En mi familia, somos cinco. Aunque somos una familia muy unida y lo pasamos

bien a menudo, de todas maneras **(1)** _____ de tensiones de vez en

cuando. Por ejemplo, mi papá trabaja mucho. Siempre regresa **(2)** _____

de la oficina. Mi mamá siempre le recomienda **(3)** _____ mejor. Mi

mamá también sufre de **(4)** _____. Es que ella también tiene mucho

trabajo. Está **(5)** _____ todo el tiempo. Tiene que trabajar y limpiar

la casa también. Y yo, como el mayor, tengo que ayudar. Mis padres siempre me dicen

"**(6)** _____." Mi hermano, en cambio, no se preocupa

mucho. Me parece que sabe **(7)** _____. Nunca se

(8) _____ nervioso ni queda **(9)** _____ como el

resto de la familia. Mi hermanito Robertín aún es muy joven. Nada más tiene cinco años.

Se **(10)** _____ frente al televisor o pasa el día jugando.

6 Briefly describe each of the following people. Use the words in the box.

> reírse mucho   sufrir de tensiones   estar rendido
>
> estar agobiado

1. El Señor Zamora se acuesta tarde y se levanta temprano. Nunca desayuna y trabaja mucho.

   _____

2. Rubén no toma las cosas con calma. Si algo le va mal comienza a sudar.

   _____

3. Clara siempre tiene mucho que hacer. Todos los días se levanta temprano, hace ejercicio, prepara el desayuno y va al trabajo. Cuando regresa del trabajo, limpia la casa.

   _____

4. Para Martín todo le parece cómico. Le gusta contar chistes y divertir a todo el mundo.

   _____

¿**Te acuerdas?** The present progressive *Pupil's Edition, p. 35*

estar + -ando Geraldo **está trabajando** ahora.

estar + -iendo **Estamos escribiendo** cartas.

7 Change each verb to the present progressive to tell what Mauro and several of his friends are doing right now.

1. Mauro y yo _____ (pasear) en velero en este momento.

2. ¿Tú _____ (leer) todas las revistas en la biblioteca?

3. Martín _____ (ver) televisión en la sala ahora mismo.

4. Javier _____ (comer) ahora el almuerzo en la cafetería con sus amigos.

5. Yo _____ (jugar) a las cartas con mis amigos.

6. María _____ (tocar) el clarinete en el concierto de orquesta.

7. Juan y María _____ (escuchar) música en el centro de recreo.

8. Tú _____ (montar) mucho a caballo.

8 Vivian needs help, but everyone she asks is busy. Fill in the blanks with the present progressive of the verbs in parentheses to say what everyone is doing.

VIVIAN ¡Hola, Mari! Oye, yo **(1)** _____ (cortar) el césped. ¿Puedes venir a ayudarme?

MARI No puedo, Vivian. Lo siento. **(2)** _____ (estudiar) para un examen que tengo mañana.

VIVIAN ¿Qué tal, Rafael? Yo **(3)** _____ (limpiar) la cocina. ¿Quieres ayudarme?

RAFAEL ¡Qué pena, Mari! Es que tengo visitas (*guests*). Ahora mismo nosotros

(4) _____ (ver) televisión.

VIVIAN Montse, yo **(5)** _____ (sacar) la basura y necesito ayuda.

MONTSE Me gustaría ayudar, Vivian, pero tengo una cita con Diego. (Él) me

(6) _____ (esperar) en el cine.

VIVIAN ¡Hola, Marcos! **(7)** _____ (buscar) a alguien que me ayude a cortar el césped. ¿Puedes?

MARCO Ay, no puedo hacerlo ahora. Es que **(8)** _____ (comer) el almuerzo con la familia.

VIVIAN Buenas tardes, Carlitos. Yo **(9)** _____ (hacer) la tarea. ¿Te gustaría venir a ayudarme?

CARLITOS Claro, Vivian. Me encantaría. ¿Puedes esperar media hora? Ahora mismo yo

(10) _____ (leer) el periódico.

CAPÍTULO 2 Primer paso

■ SEGUNDO PASO

To talk about taking care of yourself, you'll need to be able to use reflexive verbs.

¿Se te ha olvidado?   Parts of the body   *Pupil's Edition, p. 382–387*

9 Write the part of the body that you need most to do each activity.

1. escribir a máquina *(to type)* _____

2. escribir una carta _____

3. caminar _____

4. levantar pesas _____

5. escuchar música _____

6. hablar _____

7. oler *(to smell)* _____

8. leer un libro _____

---

*G*ramática de repaso   Reflexive verbs   *Pupil's Edition, p. 41*

Many verbs can be used reflexively. This means that the verb includes a reflexive pronoun when it's conjugated. The verb's meaning changes slightly:

levantar   *to lift*
levantarse   *to get up* (literally *to lift oneself*)

The reflexive pronoun corresponds to the subject of the sentence.

Yo me levanto temprano.
¿A qué hora **te** levantas **tú?**

---

10 Fill in the following blanks with the correct reflexive pronoun.

1. Todos los días _____ levanto a las siete de la mañana.

2. Mis padres _____ levantan más temprano, a eso de las seis.

3. Puesto que (*since*) sólo tenemos un baño, tenemos que bañar_____ a diferentes horas.

4. Primero _____ baña mi hermana Clara porque tiene clase temprano.

5. Mientras ella _____ baña, yo _____ lavo los dientes.

6. Entonces, _____ vestimos antes de tomar el desayuno.

7. Después de desayunar, mi hermana y yo _____ vamos a la escuela.

8. Mi mamá se va al trabajo mientras mi papá _____ queda en casa.

11 Lisandro is supposed to be at work at 9:00 AM. It's now 9:20 AM and he's still in bed. For each of the following verbs, give him a logical informal (**tú**) command, affirmative or negative, depending on what you think he has time for.

1. levantarse

_____

2. dormirse otra vez

_____

3. hacer la cama

_____

4. apurarse (*hurry*)

_____

5. bañarse

_____

6. afeitarse

_____

7. desayunar

_____

8. pasar la aspiradora

_____

9. ver televisión

_____

12 Read Juan's description of his day. Fill in the blanks with the preterite of the verb in parentheses. Be sure to include the reflexive pronoun whenever necessary.

Esta mañana mis padres (1) _____ (levantar) temprano y
(2) _____ (preparar) el desayuno. A las siete, mi papá nos
(3) _____ (despertar) a mi hermana y a mí. Luego yo fui al baño.
Yo (4) _____ (quitar) las pijamas y (5) _____
(bañar). Después, mi hermana (6) _____ (pasar) media hora en
el baño porque (7) _____ (maquillar). Después de la escuela, mis
amigos y yo (8) _____ (ir) al gimnasio. Yo (9) _____
(levantar) pesas por una hora. Por fin yo (10) _____ (regresar)
a casa y (11) _____ (estudiar) un rato. Después de cenar con mi
familia, todos nosotros (12) _____ (acostar).

CAPÍTULO 2 Segundo paso

13 Rosa and Nicolás had the following conversation about staying healthy. Fill in the blanks with the correct present, preterite, command, or infinitive form of the verb in parentheses.

ROSA   Nicolás, ¿qué es lo que haces para **(1)** _____ (cuidarse)?

NICOLÁS   Bueno, **(2)** _____ (hacer) ejercicios todos los días. O

(3) _____ (correr) o voy al gimnasio a **(4)** _____ (levantar) pesas. ¿Y tú, qué haces?

ROSA   Bueno, trato de **(5)** _____ (dormir) lo suficiente. (Yo)

(6) _____ (acostarse) muy temprano todas las noches.

NICOLÁS   Pero, ¿no haces nada para **(7)** _____ (mantenerse) en forma?

¿No haces ejercicio? ¿Cuánto tiempo **(8)** _____ (quedarse) tú frente a la tele anoche?

ROSA   Bueno, no por mucho. De todas maneras (*anyway*), yo **(9)** _____ (sentirse) muy bien. Nunca me enfermo.

NICOLÁS   Sí, pero eso no lo es todo. Además de estar a dieta, tienes que hacer ejercicio todos

los días para **(10)** _____ (cuidarse). Ayer fui a levantar pesas al

gimnasio, y vuelvo mañana. ¡No **(11)** _____ (quedarse) en la casa! ¡Ven conmigo!

VOCABULARIO   Para cuidarse la salud   *Pupil's Edition, p. 42*

14 Fill in the following conversation with an appropriate expression from the box. Conjugate any verbs as necessary.

> subir   pesarse   el peso   crema protectora
>
> broncearse   cuenta   ducharse   dormirse

BERTA   Oye, Alberto, voy a la playa esta tarde. ¿Me quieres acompañar?

ALBERTO   No, gracias. Voy al gimnasio. Esta mañana **(1)** _____ y me di

(2) _____ de que **(3)** _____ de peso.

BERTA   Ah, sí. Bueno, no hay que preocuparse. ¿Con qué frecuencia

(4) _____?

ALBERTO   Me peso todos los días.

BERTA   Al cuidarte **(5)** _____, debes pesarte una vez por semana.

ALBERTO   Tienes razón. Oye, vas a la playa con Luz esta tarde, ¿no? No te olvides de ponerte

(6) _____. Recuerda lo que te pasó la vez pasada.

BERTA   Sí, me acuerdo. **(7)** _____ bajo el sol y me quemé. Esta vez

espero **(8)** _____ bien.

15 Fill in the blanks in each sentence. Use the correct form of an appropriate verb from the word box.

ponerse	pesarse	quemarse	subir	ducharse

1. Cada vez que va a la playa, Carla _____ crema protectora para protegerse la piel.

2. Martín _____ ayer y se dio cuenta de que _____ de peso.

3. Ana tenía prisa esta mañana. Entonces, no se bañó sino que (*but*) _____.

4. Si te duermes en la playa, puedes _____.

---

*G*ramática de repaso   The imperfect   *Pupil's Edition, p. 43*

1. Verbs conjugated in the imperfect can indicate the following:

   • That an action took place on a regular basis in the past.

   • That the action was in progress when something interrupted it.
      Martín y yo **dormíamos** cuando pegó el terremoto (*earthquake*).

   • That two actions were going on at the same time. Both verbs are in the imperfect connected with **mientras**.
      Mi papá **lavaba** los platos mientras mi mamá los **secaba**.

   • To tell time in the past.
      Eran las siete de la noche.

2. There are no stem changes of any kind in the imperfect:
      d**ue**rmo → dormía   emp**ie**za → empezaba   p**i**den → pedían

---

16 Change the verbs in parentheses to the imperfect.

1. Yo _____ (levantarse) temprano todos los días.

2. Gabriela siempre _____ (pedir) una hamburguesa con queso.

3. Tú siempre _____ (comer) con tus amigos en el café.

4. A mis amigos y a mí nos _____ (gustar) mucho dar un paseo por el parque.

5. Después de las clases nosotros _____ (ir) todos a un restaurante a tomar algo.

6. Nosotros _____ (ver) mucha televisión los fines de semana.

7. De noche, tú _____ (estudiar) en la biblioteca por dos horas.

8. Yo _____ (dormir) ocho horas cada noche.

9. Abuelita _____ (venir) a visitarnos cada mes.

10. Nuestros amigos _____ (hacer) fiestas los viernes.

17 Diego is talking to his grandmother about what things used to be like when she was young. Fill in their conversation with the correct imperfect form of the verb in parentheses.

DIEGO   Abuela, ¿cómo (1) _____ (ser) las cosas cuando eras niña?

ABUELA   Bueno, no (2) _____ (haber) tanta gente ni tantos coches.

DIEGO   ¿Cómo (3) _____ (viajar) la gente sin coche?

ABUELA   Uno caminaba más. Además, la gente (4) _____ (vivir) más cerca de la ciudad.

DIEGO   ¿Dónde vivían tú y abuelo?

ABUELA   Nosotros (5) _____ (tener) una casa casi en el centro de la

ciudad, cerca de la plaza. Yo (6) _____ (levantarse) todos los

días a las siete e (7) _____ (ir) al mercado a comprar la comida.

DIEGO   ¿Y qué (8) _____ (hacer) abuelo?

ABUELA   Bueno, él trabajaba en el puerto así que él (9) _____ (levantarse) muy temprano para ir allí.

DIEGO   ¿Cómo (10) _____ (divertirse) Uds.?

ABUELA   En esos días no se veía mucha televisión así que leíamos,

(11) _____ (dar) un paseo o visitábamos a los vecinos. También

nos (12) _____ (gustar) nada más quedarnos en casa a conversar. Lo pasábamos muy bien.

18 Chela and Juanito are remembering when the electricity went out for a day last year. Use the cues provided to write what everybody was doing when the lights went out.

1. ser las ocho de la noche

   _____

2. Martín / estar en el baño

   _____

3. nuestro hermanito / dormir en su cama

   _____

4. nuestros amigos y yo / comer en el café en el centro

   _____

5. nuestros padres / ir al mercado

   _____

6. abuelita / leer un libro en la sala

   _____

7. yo / ver televisión

   _____

CAPÍTULO 3 El ayer y el mañana

PRIMER PASO

To talk about what has happened, you'll need to use the present perfect tense; you'll also need to talk about things that have changed.

VOCABULARIO   La vida moderna   *Pupil's Edition, p. 63*

1 For each of the following sets of words, write the word that doesn't belong.

_____	**1.** la autopista	la calle	la desventaja
_____	**2.** el tráfico	a la vez	en seguida
_____	**3.** los adelantos	la videocasetera	el contestador
_____	**4.** el año	la computación	el siglo
_____	**5.** el rascacielos	el edificio	la ventaja
_____	**6.** el tráfico	la tecnología	los coches
_____	**7.** en seguida	la tecnología	los adelantos
_____	**8.** adaptarse	el siglo	cambiar

2 Fill in the blanks in the following paragraph with an appropriate word from the word box.

siglos	videocasetera	computadora	tecnología	diarias
ventajas	a la vez	teléfono celular	contestador	se adapta

Ha habido muchos cambios en nuestro mundo. La **(1)** _____ ha creado

muchos aparatos que hacen más fácil nuestras vidas **(2)** _____. Por ejemplo,
hace 20 años, si uno no estaba en casa cuando sonaba el teléfono, perdía la llamada. Hoy

en día, el **(3)** _____ guarda todos nuestros mensajes. Hace veinte años, si
uno no estaba en casa para ver un programa de televisión, se lo perdía. Pero hoy en día, la

(4) _____ puede grabar un programa para que lo veamos después. Además,

es posible grabar un programa **(5)** _____ que estás viendo otro. Antes,
teníamos que usar una máquina de escribir para hacer trabajos. Hoy en día, podemos hacer

trabajos fácilmente con la **(6)** _____. Es muy interesante lo rápido que uno

(7) _____ a todos estos adelantos.

Uno se pregunta qué es lo que nos espera en los años y **(8)** _____ que vienen.

3 For each of the following sets of words, choose the letter of the word that best completes each set.

MODELO   la mano: el brazo:: el pie: **la pierna**
     a. el caballo   **c.** el perro
     b. la pierna   **d.** el tenedor

_____ **1.** la videocasetera: la televisión::el estéreo: _____
     a. la ventaja   **c.** la radio
     b. la vida diaria   **d.** el siglo

_____ **2.** el año: el siglo:: el piso: _____
     a. la tecnología   **c.** la videocasetera
     b. el rascacielos   **d.** el teléfono

_____ **3.** la ventaja: la desventaja::mejorar: _____
     a. adaptarse   **c.** el contestador
     b. informar   **d.** empeorar

_____ **4.** la calle: la autopista::la casa: _____
     a. el siglo   **c.** la vida diaria
     b. el rascacielos   **d.** el año

_____ **5.** el contestador: el teléfono::la videocasetera: _____
     a. la televisión   **c.** la desventaja
     b. la tecnología   **d.** la vida diaria

_____ **6.** la computadora: el ordenador::la computación: _____
     a. la autopista   **c.** la contestadora
     b. la informática   **d.** la ventaja

_____ **7.** la tecnología: la computadora::la arquitectura: _____
     a. la vida diaria   **c.** empeorar
     b. el siglo   **d.** el rascacielos

_____ **8.** a la vez: en seguida::hoy en día: _____
     a. el rascacielos   **c.** la ventaja
     b. el mañana   **d.** el siglo

¿Se te ha olvidado?   Object pronouns   *Pupil's Edition, pp. 336–356*

4 Fill in Mateo and Silvia's conversation with an appropriate object pronoun (**me, te, lo, la,** etc.).

MATEO   Oye, Silvia. Ven a ver mi nuevo contestador. Es muy interesante.

SILVIA   ¿Un contestador? ¿Por qué **(1)** _____ compraste?

MATEO   Ayer **(2)** _____ llamó María tres veces cuando no estaba. Mi hermano no me escribió ningún recado. Ahora María está enojada porque no **(3)** _____ llamé.

SILVIA   Bueno, María no se queda enojada por mucho tiempo. Además, ella te ve a menudo (*often*). ¿Por qué **(4)** _____ llama tantas veces?

MATEO   No sé. Creo que **(5)** _____ echa de menos.

SILVIA   Bueno, Mateo me gustaría ver tu contestador pero no puedo. **(6)** _____ veo otro día.

5 In the following sentences, rewrite each of the underlined phrases replacing any repetitive words with a pronoun. Remember that object pronouns are placed directly in front of the conjugated verb or can be attached to the end of an infinitive or affirmative command.

MODELO   Hay mucho tráfico, <u>pero podemos bajar el tráfico si manejamos menos nuestros coches.</u>
pero podemos bajarlo si manejamos menos nuestros coches.

1. Diego quiere usar el teléfono celular, <u>pero no puede encontrar el teléfono celular.</u>

_____

2. Los rascacielos son altísimos, por eso no <u>construimos los rascacielos aquí.</u>

_____

3. Yo sé que los teléfonos celulares están muy de moda; <u>de todos modos no me gusta usar los teléfonos celulares.</u>

_____

4. Esta computadora es muy buena. <u>¡Compra la computadora!</u>

_____

5. Los adelantos que se notan en este mundo son obvios. <u>Podemos ver los adelantos inmediatamente.</u>

_____

6. Es buena idea construir más autopistas <u>pero sólo si necesitamos las autopistas.</u>

_____

7. Me encanta el horno de microondas. <u>Uso el horno de microondas todos los días.</u>

_____

6 Claudia is asking for your advice. Answer her questions using informal commands with direct object pronouns. Remember to attach pronouns to the end of affirmative commands or to place them before negative commands.

MODELO   ¿Veo esa película? (no)   **No, no la veas.**

1. ¿Compro la computadora? (sí)

_____

2. ¿Pongo la mesa ahora? (no)

_____

3. ¿Uso la videocasetera para grabar *(record)* ese programa? (no)

_____

4. ¿Hago la cama ahora? (sí)

_____

5. ¿Lavo los platos? (sí)

_____

6. ¿Preparo las tortas para esta noche? (sí)

_____

Gramática   The present perfect   *Pupil's Edition, p. 64*

- In English when you say *I have done something* or *He has done something*, you are using the present perfect tense—the present tense of *to have* plus the past participle of the verb (*done, eaten, seen,* etc.).
- The present perfect in Spanish is the same—the present tense of **haber** (*have*) plus the past participle of the verb. The past participle in Spanish is formed by dropping the -**ar**, -**er**, or -**ir** of the infinitive and adding -**ado** if it's an -**ar** verb (**adaptado**) and by adding -**ido** if it's an -**er**, or -**ir** verb (**leído, repetido**). Here is the conjugation of **haber comprado** *(to have bought)*.

yo **he comprado**	nosotros **hemos comprado**
tú **has comprado**	vosotros habéis comprado
él / ella / Ud. **ha comprado**	ellos / ellas / Uds. **han comprado**

Some past participles are irregular. They are listed on page 64 of your textbook.

7 Martín is writing a report about what has happened in his home town. He has the following notes. Fill in the blank with the correct form of **haber**.

1. Nuestra ciudad _____ cambiado bastante. Todo es diferente.

2. Antes, la gente andaba mucho a pie. Pero (ellos) _____ construido muchas autopistas, así se maneja más.

3. Nosotros _____ aprendido mucho sobre el medio ambiente.

4. La gente _____ decidido tratar de protegerlo.

5. Mis amigos y yo _____ organizado un club de ecología.

6. Yo solo _____ sembrado cinco árboles.

8 Below is the report Martín wrote based on his notes. Fill in each of the blanks with the correct form of the past participle of the verb in parentheses.

La ciudad de Martinilla no fue siempre la ciudad que es hoy. Ha **(1)** _____ (haber) muchos cambios. Por ejemplo, en 1985, el ayuntamiento pasó una ley para el

mejoramiento de la ciudad. Desde entonces, la gente ha **(2)** _____ (cambiar)

mucho. Por ejemplo, muchas personas han **(3)** _____ (comenzar) a usar el

transporte público en vez de manejar sus coches. También han **(4)** _____ (poner) basureros en las esquinas. Además, nosotros los estudiantes hemos

(5) _____ (abrir) un centro de reciclaje. Antes la gente botaba toda la

basura a la calle. Ahora han **(6)** _____ (descubrir) que es fácil reciclar y así uno conserva muchos recursos naturales.

Aunque queda mucho por hacer, es cierto que ya hemos **(7)** _____ (hacer)

mucho. Hemos **(8)** _____ (ver) con nuestros ojos que podemos hacer un cambio.

CAPÍTULO 3 Primer paso

9 Conjugate the verbs in parentheses in the present perfect.

1. María Inés ya no está. Creo que ya _____ (irse).

2. Ella me _____ (decir) varias veces que se siente mal.

3. Yo le _____ (escribir) tres cartas este mes.

4. Ella no me _____ (contestar) ninguna.

5. Nosotros _____ (decidir) no molestarla si quiere estar sola.

6. Ella _____ (hacer) esto antes y siempre sale bien.

¿Te acuerdas?   Expressions with the present perfect   *Pupil's Edition, p. 64*

10 Adriana's friend Rosana is in New York on vacation. In this conversation, Adriana is asking her what she has and hasn't done there. Fill in each blank with **ya, alguna vez,** or **todavía.**

ADRIANA   Hola, Rosana, ¿te gusta Nueva York? ¿Qué has hecho **(1)** _____?

ROSANA   Lo estoy pasando muy bien. Hoy fui a la Estatua de la Libertad pero

   (2) _____ no he visto el Museo de la Historia Natural.

ADRIANA   Tienes que ver el Edificio del "Empire State". Es muy impresionante.

ROSANA   Sí, lo sé. La próxima vez que yo venga a Nueva York, tienes que acompañarme.

   ¿**(3)** _____ has visto Nueva York?

ADRIANA   No, nunca, y **(4)** _____ quiero verlo. ¡Tal vez el año que viene!

¿Se te ha olvidado?   Affirmatives and negatives   *Pupil's Edition, p. 382–397*

11 Claudia and Enrique are twins, but they're complete opposites. They only agree on two things: neither one of them likes Brussels sprouts and they both like basketball. With that in mind, for each sentence that describes Claudia, write a sentence saying what is probably true for Enrique, and vice versa.

MODELO   Claudia nunca hace su tarea.   **Enrique siempre la hace.**

1. Enrique nunca se acuesta temprano.

   _____

2. Enrique sabe mucho de la música.

   _____

3. A Enrique le gustaría ir a la playa o al lago.

   _____

4. A Enrique no le gustan las coles de Bruselas (*Brussels sprouts*).

   _____

5. A Claudia le encanta el baloncesto.

   _____

CAPÍTULO 3 Primer paso

■ SEGUNDO PASO

To talk about future events, you'll need to use the future tense.

*G*ramática   The future tense   *Pupil's Edition, p. 71*

The future tense is formed by adding the future endings to the future stem of the verb: **-é, -ás, -á, -emos, -án**. The infinitive serves as the future stem for all verbs except those listed on page 71 of your textbook. Beyond those irregular verbs, there are no other stem changes in the future tense.

yo **dormiré**	nosotros **dormiremos**
tú **dormirás**	vosotros dormiréis
él / ella / Ud. **dormirá**	ellos / ellas / Uds. **dormirán**

12 Change the verbs in parentheses from present tense to future.

1. El avión _____ (salir) mañana a las dos de la tarde.

2. El vuelo _____ (llegar) a San Antonio a las cuatro y media.

3. Todos nuestros familiares _____ (estar) muy contentos de vernos.

4. En San Antonio mis primos y yo _____ (ir) a muchos lugares turísticos.

5. Si tú vienes con nosotros, _____ (divertirse).

6. Mis abuelos _____ (venir) a San Antonio también.

7. Ellos también _____ (ponerse) muy contentos.

8. _____ (haber) mucho que hacer allí en San Antonio.

13 Margo is thinking about what her future will be like. For each phrase, write a question using the future tense of the verb in parentheses.

MODELO   *my future career* (dedicarse)   **¿A qué me dedicaré?**

1. *where I'll be able to travel* (poder) _____

2. *what college I'll go to* (asistir) _____

3. *where I'll meet new friends* (conocer) _____

4. *what my friends will study* (estudiar) _____

5. *who my professors will be* (ser) _____

6. *where I'll live (*vivir) _____

7. *number of children I will have* (tener) _____

CAPÍTULO 3 Segundo paso

14 Matilde was working on the following report for her social studies class about the future. Fill in the blanks with the correct future tense form of the verb in parentheses.

En el futuro **(1)** _____ (haber) muchos cambios y el mundo del futuro

(2) _____ (ser) muy distinto al de hoy. Por ejemplo, la computadora

(3) _____ (tener) un lugar aún más importante. Hoy usamos mucho

las computadoras, pero en el futuro las **(4)** _____ (usar) más. El uso de la

computadora **(5)** _____ (cambiar) la manera en que nos comunicamos. Nosotros

(6) _____ (hablar) tanto por computadora como por teléfono y hasta las noticias las

(7) _____ (leer) por la computadora.

Otro cambio **(8)** _____ (tener) lugar en el transporte. En el futuro la gente

(9) _____ (manejar) carros eléctricos que no **(10)** _____ (contaminar)

el aire. También se **(11)** _____ (tomar) más el autobús y otras formas de transporte

público. De esta manera no **(12)** _____ (haber) tanta contaminación como hoy.

Es cierto que nuestra vida diaria **(13)** _____ (cambiar) en el futuro. Tenemos

que prepararnos para estos cambios. De esta manera **(14)** _____ (estar) listos
cuando lleguen.

15 Write a sentence saying what you think will probably happen to each person or what they will probably do next.

1. María estudió por tres horas. Está muy cansada. Entonces . . .

   _____

2. Sé que tú no has comido nada hoy. Acabas de salir de tu última clase. Entonces probablemente . . .

   _____

3. Hace mucho calor hoy y Julia está corriendo. Cuando llegue a casa . . .

   _____

4. Alejandro suspendió el examen de química. La próxima vez . . .

   _____

5. Necesito más dinero para asistir a la universidad. Este verano . . .

   _____

6. Está muy nublado hoy. Pronosticaron lluvia así que dentro de un rato . . .

   _____

7. Felipe está muy aburrido hoy. Pero lo invitaron sus amigos a salir así que . . .

   _____

8. A Sandra le encanta la Argentina. Algún día . . .

   _____

CAPÍTULO 3 Segundo paso

¿Te acuerdas?   Making comparisons   *Pupil's Edition, p. 72*

más . . . que *more . . . than*	tan . . . como *as . . . as*
menos . . . que *less . . . than* tanto(os/a/as) . . . como	*as much (many) . . . as*

16 Alani has taken an informal survey about how many things people in her class have done. Complete the sentences below according to the chart. Fill in the first blank with **más**, **menos**, or the correct form of **tanto**, and the second with either **que** or **como**.

	Amanda	Robertín	Chen	Ángelo	Kirk	Jodi
películas	22	21	4	3	9	12
ciudades	1	1	1	3	2	5
comidas	3	9	2	1	1	10
fiestas	2	2	4	1	2	3

1. Amanda ha visto _____ películas _____ Chen.

2. Robertín ha viajado a _____ ciudades _____ Amanda.

3. Kirk ha ido a _____ fiestas _____ Amanda.

4. Jodi ha probado (*tasted*) _____ comidas _____ Kirk.

5. Jodi ha visto _____ películas _____ Robertín.

6. Chen ha ido a _____ ciudades _____ Kirk.

17 Use the following cues to write complete logical sentences. You will need to add **más**, **menos**, the correct form of **tanto**, and either **que** or **como**.

MODELO   enero / tener / días / febrero   **Enero tiene más días que febrero.**

1. la pizza / tener / calorías / la manzana

   _____

2. el siglo / tener / años / la década (*decade*)

   _____

3. el coche / tener / ruedas / la bicicleta

   _____

4. el perro / tener / piernas / el gato

   _____

5. el lago / ser / grande / el océano

   _____

¿Te acuerdas? Vamos a + infinitive *Pupil's Edition, p. 73*

18 Javier is trying to get his friends to do things with him. What do you think Javier would say to his friends to get them to all go together? Use **vamos a** + *infinitive*.

1. Tengo hambre.

   _____

2. Hay una nueva película en el cine.

   _____

3. Hace muy buen tiempo hoy y hay mucha gente en el parque.

   _____

4. Hace sol y la piscina está abierta.

   _____

5. Aprendí un baile nuevo.

   _____

6. Tenemos un examen de química muy difícil.

   _____

VOCABULARIO   El futuro   *Pupil's Edition, p. 73*

19 The following is an excerpt from this month's issue of **El mañana** magazine. Fill in the blanks with an appropriate word from the word box. Conjugate any verbs as necessary.

botar	carros eléctricos	desarrollar	porvenir
destruir		energía solar	mejorar

En el mundo de hoy, la tecnología ha causado muchos problemas que todavía tenemos que resolver. Tal vez el problema más grave sea el de la contaminación. De todas maneras, hay mucho que podemos hacer para (1) _____ la situación. En primer lugar, podemos (2) _____ nuevas formas de energía. La (3) _____, por ejemplo, es una forma de energía muy limpia que no (4) _____ el medio ambiente. Y además el sol vivirá por muchos años más. Otra cosa que podemos hacer es comenzar a manejar (5) _____. También nos toca reciclar la basura. Hasta ahora hemos (6) _____ mucha basura.

CAPÍTULO 3 Segundo paso

CAPÍTULO 4

Alrededor de la mesa

■ PRIMER PASO

To talk about how food tastes, you'll need to know the names of various foods. You might also need to know how to describe things emphatically with the **-ísimo** ending. To talk about unintentional events, you'll need to use reflexive verbs with indirect object pronouns.

¿Te acuerdas?   Absolute superlatives   *Pupil's Edition, p. 89*

1 Fill in the blanks in the following dialogues with the **-ísimo** form of the adjectives in parentheses. Watch out for spelling changes.

1.   CELINA   ¿Qué te parece esta canción, Mari?

     MARI   Me gusta mucho. Es _____ (bueno).

2.   CARLOS   ¿Te gusta la clase de latín, Felipe?

     FELIPE   Para nada. Es _____ (aburrido).

     CARLOS   Pero el profesor es _____ (simpático), ¿no?

3.   BEATRIZ   ¿Quieren ir a comer al Café Santos?

     MARCOS   Cómo no. ¡La comida es _____ (rico)!

     BEATRIZ   De acuerdo. Sirven unos postres que son _____ (caro).

4. FEDERICO   Yolanda, ¿has leído *Cien años de soledad*?

     YOLANDA   N'hombre. Es _____ (largo).

5.   MARIO   ¿Por qué no quieren venir ni Elena ni Chela?

     ESTRELLA   Regresaron del gimnasio y están _____ (cansado).

6.   ADELA   ¿Cómo saliste en el examen, María?

     MARÍA   Saqué una A. ¡Estoy _____ (contento)!

2 Use the **-ísimo** form of an appropriate adjective to describe these things.

1. la tarea _____

2. la comida de la cafetería _____

3. los cuentos de hadas _____

4. el fútbol _____

5. la música clásica _____

6. la clase de español _____

VOCABULARIO   La comida   *Pupil's Edition, p. 90*

3 Use the vocabulary on page 90 of your textbook to organize the menu at Fonda San Diego, a new restaurant. Place the various dishes for the day in the correct category on the menu.

Fonda San Diego
Entremeses (appetizers)

_____

_____

Platos principales
Carnes

_____

_____

_____

Pescados y mariscos

_____

_____

Postres
Frutas

_____

_____

4 For each of the following groups of words, choose the word that doesn't belong and write it in the blank.

_____	1. el bacalao	los melocotones	la trucha
_____	2. el bistec	la piña	los melocotones
_____	3. la ternera	el chorizo	el pargo
_____	4. las almejas	la ensalada	las ostras
_____	5. el bacalao	la patilla	el ananás
_____	6. la torta	la trucha	el quesillo
_____	7. el pollo frito	el bistec a la parrilla	las caraotas
_____	8. los frijoles negros	la torta	las legumbres

5 You're planning a five-course meal for four people who have special dietary needs. Victoria is a vegetarian and is allergic to dairy products. Simón doesn't like seafood. Diego doesn't eat red meat or pork and doesn't like seafood. Sandra loves seafood but not shellfish. She's also allergic to chocolate. You have the following items available. Write what five items you'll serve each person.

| ensalada mixta | patilla | bacalao | arroz | pollo a la parrilla | quesillo |
| torta de chocolate | | almejas | bistec a la parrilla | | caraotas |

	Victoria	Simón	Diego	Sandra
entremés				
plato principal				
segundo				
tercero				
postre				

*G*ramática   se + indirect object pronouns   *Pupil's Edition, p. 91*

Spanish often uses reflexive verbs like **caerse, perderse,** and **romperse** to talk about accidents and other things that happen unintentionally.

El vaso **se** rompió.   *The glass broke.*

In sentences that talk about accidents, the subject of the sentence (**el vaso**) is usually placed at the end, and the person it happened to is preceded by **a** and most often placed at the beginning:

A Carmen se le rompió el vaso.   *Carmen broke the glass.*

6 In each of the following sentences, conjugate the verb in parentheses in the preterite. Make sure the verb agrees with the subject of the sentence.

1. A Jaime se le _____ (perder) los libros.

2. Se nos _____ (quedar) las llaves en el carro.

3. Estas chuletas que preparé no están buenas. Se me _____ (quemar).

4. Ya no tenemos nada de leche. Se nos _____ (acabar) esta mañana.

5. ¿A ti se te _____ (romper) el vaso?

6. ¿Cómo pasó? ¿Se te _____ (caer) de la mano?

7. A Jesús y a Sara se les _____ (olvidar) la fecha del cumpleaños de su mamá.

7 The counselor at Camp Browder is telling you about the following mishaps on the first day. Fill in the blanks with the correct indirect object pronoun (**me**, **te**, **le**, etc.) to indicate who the following unintentional events happened to.

A Claudia se (1) _____ rompieron los lentes y no podía leer.

A mi hermana y a mí se (2) _____ descompuso el coche en camino al campamento. ¿No me dijiste, Pablo, que no podías manejar tu coche porque se (3) _____ perdieron las llaves? Marcos y Rosana no sacaron ninguna foto porque se (4) _____ quedó la cámara en casa. Hoy no pude comer cereal para el desayuno porque se (5) _____ acabó la leche. Linda estaba muy distraída. Se (6) _____ olvidaron los libros. Esta mañana a ti se (7) _____ acabó la gasolina. Amparo siempre tiene mucho cuidado en la cocina. Por ejemplo, nunca se (8) _____ ha roto ningún plato. Elena fue muy torpe en la cocina. A ella se (9) _____ quemaron las chuletas.

8 Bárbara and Julio are talking about today's Latin test. Fill in the blanks in their conversation with **se** and the correct indirect object pronoun.

BÁRBARA Hola, Julio. ¿Cómo saliste en el examen de latín?

JULIO Ay, pésimo. Déjame decirte lo que pasó. Juan se sentó junto a mí e hizo muchísimo

ruido. (A él) **(1)** _____ cayeron los papeles varias veces.

BÁRBARA Pero el examen…

JULIO Sí, sí. Primero al comenzar, a mi bolígrafo **(2)** _____ acabó la

tinta (*ink*). Entonces quise usar lápiz pero a mí **(3)** _____ rompió.

Durante el examen, a mí **(4)** _____ olvidó la conjugación
del verbo *ferre*. Pero creo que salí bastante bien. A propósito, Profesor Moore dijo
que podíamos usar un diccionario.

BÁRBARA Ay, no. Tengo el mismo examen hoy y no traigo el mío (*mine*). Es que (a mí)

(5) _____ quedó en casa.

JULIO Bueno, no puedo darte mi diccionario porque (a mí) **(6)** _____
perdió. Lo siento.

9 Celia had a really tough day! Fill in the blanks with the correct forms of the verbs from the word box to describe the unintentional events that happened.

| olvidarse | acabarse | descomponerse | quedarse | romperse | perderse |

Hoy fue un desastre. Primero quedé dormido hasta las nueve. Tengo clase a las ocho y media. Me vestí rápidamente y salí corriendo. Mientras manejaba a la escuela,

(1) _____ la gasolina. Mi papá usó el coche ayer y

(2) _____ llenar el tanque. Tuve que dejar el coche y seguir

caminando. Mientras caminaba, (3) _____ la camisa en un árbol. Llegué tarde a mi primera clase y entonces me di cuenta de que

(4) _____ la tarea en casa.

10 Using the cues below, write sentences to tell about various happenings in the Sabater household. Use the tense indicated in parentheses.

1. a Felipe / descomponerse / el coche / ayer *(preterite)*

   _____

   _____

2. a nosotras / todavía no / acabarse / la leche *(present perfect)*

   _____

   _____

3. a Julián / ya / perderse / los lentes / tres veces *(present perfect)*

   _____

   _____

4. de niña / a Margarita / olvidarse / hacer la cama / muchas veces *(imperfect)*

   _____

   _____

5. siempre / (a mí) / romperse / los platos / cuando / (yo) cocinar *(present or imperfect)*

   _____

   _____

6. a Jaimito / siempre / acabarse / la gasolina / porque / nunca / (él) llenar / el tanque *(present or imperfect)*

   _____

   _____

7. A Evelyn / caerse / el tenedor / durante el desayuno *(preterite)*

   _____

   _____

■ SEGUNDO PASO

When asking for help and requesting favors, you might ask someone to run errands. To do this, you'll need to know the names of various stores and how to use various expressions with **por** and **para**. You may also need to use direct and indirect object pronouns together.

Nota *G*ramatical   **por** and **para**   *Pupil's Edition, p. 96*

You've learned the word **por** in expressions like **por la mañana**, **por fin**, **por favor**, and **por ejemplo**. The word **por** is also used in the following ways:

   in exchange for—pagar **por**
   for a period of time—**por** tres días
   by—pasar **por** tu casa; escrito **por** shakespeare; **por** avión

You've learned to use **para** in expressions like **para mí**. The word **para** is also used in the following ways:

   intended for—escrito **para** estudiantes
   in order to / for the purpose of—arroz **para** preparar la sopa

---

11 Complete each of the following sentences with **por** or **para**.

1. Hoy _____ la mañana me levanté temprano.

2. Ayer Mario me habló a las siete _____ teléfono.

3. No pude desayunar porque se me acabó la leche _____ el cereal.

4. Después de esperar _____ media hora, _____ fin llegó el autobús.

5. ¿_____ favor, mamá, me puedes llevar al cine esta tarde?

6. Todavía no estoy lista _____ salir. ¿Me esperas _____ un momento?

12 Fill in Maribel and Robertín's conversation with either **por** or **para**.

MARIBEL   Oye, Robertín, ¿me ayudas a lavar los platos, (**1**) _____ favor?

ROBERTÍN   Claro, pero ¿puedes esperar (**2**) _____ un minuto? Tengo que acabar

   la tarea (**3**) _____ mi clase de química.

MARIBEL   ¿(**4**) _____ qué no la hiciste esta mañana?

ROBERTÍN   Es que tuve que hacer muchas cosas esta mañana. (**5**) _____ ejemplo,

   tuve que pasar (**6**) _____ la librería (**7**) _____ comprar un

   libro (**8**) _____ mamá.

MARIBEL   Entonces, ¿estás haciéndola ahora?

ROBERTÍN   Sí, ¡(**9**) _____ fin!

VOCABULARIO   Tiendas   *Pupil's Edition, p. 97*

13 Sr. Sifuentes doesn't know what stores to go to for the items on his list. Write each item on his list in the appropriate column so he'll know where to go for each one.

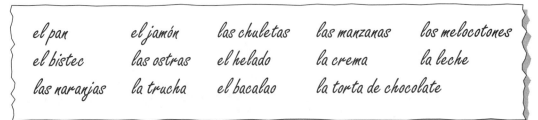

el pan	el jamón	las chuletas	las manzanas	los melocotones
el bistec	las ostras	el helado	la crema	la leche
las naranjas	la trucha	el bacalao	la torta de chocolate	

la lechería	la carnicería	la panadería	la pastelería
_____	_____	_____	_____
_____	_____	_____	_____
_____	_____	_____	_____

la frutería	la heladería	la pescadería
_____	_____	_____
_____	_____	_____
_____	_____	_____

14 You want to buy the following things but don't have time to go shopping. As each person tells you where they're going, answer by asking him or her to buy you what you need.

MODELO   Voy a la ferretería.   **¿Me puedes comprar un martillo?**

✔ un martillo *(hammer)*	un litro de leche	medio kilo de melocotones
unos clavos *(nails)*	medio kilo de mantequilla	un kilo de carne
helado de vainilla	pan francés	

1. Julia y yo vamos a la frutería.

_____

2. Voy a la lechería. ¿Te compro algo?

_____

3. Pienso ir a la ferretería esta tarde. ¿Necesitas algo?

_____

4. Voy a pasar por la carnicería hoy. ¿Qué te compro?

_____

5. ¿Qué te puedo comprar en la panadería?

_____

*G*ramática   Double object pronouns   *Pupil's Edition, p. 98*

When a sentence has both a direct and indirect object pronoun, the indirect object pronoun always comes before the direct object pronoun:

Sergio me regaló el libro. Sergio **me lo** regaló ayer.

Si necesitas dinero, yo te presto el dinero. Yo **te lo** presto.

The indirect object pronouns **le** and **les** change to **se** when they come before the direct object pronouns **lo, la, los,** and **las.**

Papá necesita las llaves del carro. ¿**Se las** das?

Pronouns come immediately before a conjugated verb or can be attached to an infinitive or to an affirmative command. Wherever they appear, though, the two pronouns always stay next to each other and in the same order:

¿**Me los** pueden comprar? ¿Pueden comprár**melos**?

When object pronouns are attached to a word, an accent mark is added over the stressed syllable:

¡Cómpra**melos**!

15 Fill in the blank with the correct direct object pronoun (**me, te, lo, la, nos, los,** or **las**).

1. ¿Te gusta la camisa? _____ compré ayer en el centro comercial.

2. ¿Por qué no viniste a mi fiesta, Tomás? _____ invité la semana pasada.

3. Carolina _____ llamó por teléfono esta mañana pero yo no estaba en casa.

4. Raquel no tiene los boletos. _____ perdió en el colegio.

5. No tengo tiempo para ver las fotos. _____ veo más tarde.

6. Mi abuela va a estar con nosotros durante el mes de julio. Siempre _____ visita en el verano.

7. ¿No encuentras tu libro de matemáticas? _____ vi en el coche.

16 Fill in the following blanks with **le, les,** or **se.**

1.   PAPÁ   Se nos acabó el pastel. _____ serví el último pedazo a Mari.

     JOSÉ   ¿Qué tal la fruta? _____ la serviste a Mari también, ¿no?

     PAPÁ   No. Ella no la quería. _____ di nada más el pastel.

2.   MARI   ¿Ya _____ has comprado un regalo de cumpleaños a Héctor?

     CRIS   Sí, ya _____ lo he comprado.

3.   DIEGO   Sara, ¿quieres preguntar_____ a Sandra si quiere venir con nosotros?

     SARA   Ya _____ he preguntado. No quiere venir.

4.   MARTÍN   ¿Todavía vamos a hacer_____ una fiesta a Santiago?

     FLORI   Pues, sí. Vamos a hacér_____la este sábado.

CAPÍTULO 4 Segundo paso

17 Last year you and your friends decided to exchange gifts for a holiday. Below are the gifts that you got and the names of the people that gave them to you. For each item, write a sentence explaining who gave you each of the gifts. Use the verbs **dar** and **regalar**.

MODELO   los chocolates / Pablo

¿Los chocolates? Me los dio Pablo.

1. el anillo *(ring)* / María

_____

2. los libros / tú

_____

3. la cafetera *(coffee pot)* / Santos y Carlos

_____

When you got home, your parents wanted to know who you gave gifts to. Use the following cues to explain.

MODELO   la camisa / Pablo

¿La camisa? Se la di a Pablo.

4. los discos compactos / Silvia

_____

5. la cámara / Carmen

_____

6. el estéreo / Diego y Carolina

_____

18 Fill in the blanks in the following restaurant conversation with the correct form of the direct and indirect object pronouns.

MODELO   ¿Qué hiciste con la cámara?

Se la di a Carmen.

1.   MARIO   Mamá, ¿quién nos trae la comida en este restaurante?

SILVIA   _____ _____ va a traer el camarero, hijo.

2.   KARIN   Mamá, necesito un tenedor. ¿A quién _____ _____ pido?

SILVIA   Píde_____ al camarero.

3.   SILVIA   Camarero, ¿nos podría traer cuatro vasos de agua?

CAMARERO   En seguida _____ _____ traigo.

4.   MARIO   Mamá, ¿me podría pasar el pan?

SILVIA   Claro que _____ _____ puedo pasar.

5.   KARIN   ¿Dónde está la sal?

SILVIA   _____ _____ di a tu hermano. Píde_____ a él.

Nuestras leyendas

■ PRIMER PASO

To express qualified agreement and disagreement, you'll need to know various expressions. To report what others say and think, you should be able to use impersonal expressions with **se**.

ᑌASÍ SE DICE Expressing qualified agreement   *Pupil's Edition, p. 117*
and disagreement

1 For each set of expressions, write the one that doesn't fit with the others.

_____	1. De acuerdo.	Claro que sí.	¡Qué va!
_____	2. Por supuesto.	Desde luego.	¡Qué tontería!
_____	3. ¡Al contrario!	¿Tú crees?	Claro que no.
_____	4. No sé.	¡Nada de eso!	Puede ser, pero...
_____	5. Depende.	Eso es.	Así es.
_____	6. ¡Cómo no!	¡Qué va!	¡Es muy difícil!
_____	7. Así es.	Desde luego.	Bueno, puede ser.

2 Here are the results of an opinion survey you sent out. Tally up the responses to determine whether the student body wants to buy a new school flag (**bandera**) or not.

¿Necesitamos de verdad una bandera? No sé; es muy difícil decidir.

¡Qué tontería gastar dinero en una bandera!

¡Qué va! ¿Una bandera?   Desde luego.

¿Una bandera? ¡Por supuesto!   ¡Cómo no!

Estoy de acuerdo. ¡Buena idea!   ¡Nada de banderas!

¿Una bandera? Hasta cierto punto, es necesaria, pero...

A FAVOR	INDECISO *(UNDECIDED)*	EN CONTRA

_____ Comprar la bandera   _____ No comprar la bandera

Nota *G*ramatical The impersonal **se** *Pupil's Edition, p. 119*

In a sentence about what people in general do, **se** can replace the subjects **uno, la gente, ellos,** etc. The verb usually becomes singular.

Aquí uno trabaja mucho. → Aquí **se** trabaja mucho.

Muchos creen que el mundo es redondo. → **Se** cree que el mundo es redondo.

Antes, la gente lo pasaba bien leyendo. → Antes, **se** lo pasaba bien leyendo.

¿Cómo dicen *legend* en español? → ¿Cómo **se** dice *legend* en español?

3 Rewrite each of the following sentences about Belén's school using the impersonal **se**.

MODELO   Muchas personas leen en la biblioteca.
         Se lee en la biblioteca.

1. La gente habla mucho español en la clase.

   _____

2. Mucha gente usa computadoras en las clases.

   _____

3. Las personas comen bien en la cafetería.

   _____

4. Muchos trabajan en los laboratorios de química.

   _____

5. La gente practica muchos deportes.

   _____

4 Using **se**, write questions for the following contexts.

MODELO   where people go to take a walk   **¿Adónde se va a dar un paseo?**

1. how one gets to the pharmacy

   _____

2. what people do at a party

   _____

3. where people like to go to shop

   _____

4. why people exercise

   _____

5. why people save (**ahorrar**) money

   _____

■ SEGUNDO PASO

To talk about hopes and wishes you'll need to use the subjunctive mood. You'll also need to know specific vocabulary.

VOCABULARIO   Las leyendas   *Pupil's Edition, p. 124*

5 Choose the correct completion for each of the following statements about World War II.

1. Después de que los japoneses atacaron Pearl Harbor el 7 de diciembre de 1941, los

    Estados Unidos _____.
    a. celebró la boda b. traicionó el país c. declaró la guerra

2. Los Aliados (*Allies*) celebraron su _____ después de la derrota del Eje (*Axis*).
    a. heroína b. victoria c. diosa

3. Los países aliados _____ fuertemente por vencer al ejército alemán.
    a. lucharon b. acordaron c. quedaron

4. Después de la explosión de la bomba atómica en Japón, casi 100.000 personas

    _____.
    a. traicionaron b. se regocijaron c. quedaron muertas

5. Cuando terminó la guerra, los militares se juntaron para _____.
    a. acordar la paz b. celebrar la boda c. vencer al ejército enemigo

6 The following is a legend from the Incas in South America and tells the origin of day and night. Fill in the blanks with words from the box. Conjugate any verbs as necessary.

regocijarse	quedar casi muerto	vencer	celebrar la boda	dios	malvado
	diosa		soldado		guerreros

Cuando el rey Cuyaypag y su esposa Pacarina tuvieron su primera hija, todo el pueblo

(1) _____ . Levantaron a su hija al (2) _____ del
sol, al Padre Inti, quien le puso el nombre Cuyana. Después de varios años, la princesa

Cuyana se hizo muy bella. Muchos jóvenes, soldados y (3) _____

vinieron para casarse con ella. Pero el (4) _____ Millanaypag
también quería casarse con la princesa. Para asustar a la gente se transformó en un cóndor.

Un (5) _____ , Cachashca, luchó fuertemente por

(6) _____ al cóndor pero no pudo y (7) _____
en la playa, donde Cuyana lo encontró. Inmediatamente se enamoraron y decidieron
casarse. Pero cuando el malvado Millanaypag oyó sus planes, no

(8) _____ sino que quiso destruir el reino. Padre Inti salió del
cielo para castigar a Millanaypag y hoy en día sale del cielo todos los días para castigarlo,

y mientras tanto, Quilla, la (9) _____ de la luna, vigila (*watches
over*) la tierra.

Gramática   The subjunctive mood   *Pupil's Edition, p. 126*

- To express what someone wants or hopes will happen, a phrase beginning with **que** + a verb in the subjunctive mood is used:

  Quiero **que el camarero me sirva** un refresco.

  Juan espera **que su novia lo llame** por teléfono.

- Both examples have two phrases. The first phrase is in the indicative and tells what is actual (**quiero, espera**). The second phrase, beginning with **que,** has a verb in the subjunctive and tells what someone hopes will happen or wants to happen. The two phrases have two different subjects.

  Juan espera que **Uds.** visiten.

- Sometimes the expression **ojalá** is used to express hope, as in **Ojalá que no llueva hoy.**

- The present subjunctive is formed by dropping the **-o** of the yo form of the present tense of the verb and adding the following endings.

HABLAR

que **hable**	que **hablemos**
que **hables**	que habléis
que **hable**	que **hablen**

COMER

que **coma**	que **comamos**
que **comas**	que comáis
que **coma**	que **coman**

7 Fill in the blanks in the following paragraph with either the present indicative or the present subjunctive of the verbs in parentheses.

Ayer en la escuela oí que nosotros (1) _____ (ir) a estudiar

las leyendas. Estoy muy emocionada porque me (2) _____

(gustar) mucho las leyendas. Alguien me ha dicho que las leyendas

(3) _____ (ser) aburridas, pero no estoy de acuerdo. Espero que

nosotros (4) _____ (estudiar) las leyendas de la religión azteca.

Me fascinan. Por ejemplo, dicen que Quetzalcóatl (5) _____ (ser) el

dios de la civilización y del aprender. Quiero saber más de él. Otros estudiantes dicen

que la religión azteca (6) _____ (ser) poco interesante. Quieren

que nosotros (7) _____ (comenzar) a estudiar las leyendas

romanas. Espero que el profesor no les (8) _____ (hacer) caso

porque ya sé mucho de las leyendas romanas. Ojalá que los otros estudiantes

(9) _____ (aprender) algo de la religión azteca.

8 Fill in each of the following blanks with the present subjunctive of the verb in parentheses.

1. Hoy tenemos una fiesta. Espero que todos _____ (venir).

2. Mis padres quieren que nosotros _____ (comenzar) temprano.

3. También quiero que todos _____ (traer) su música favorita.

4. Vamos a preparar mucha comida. Ojalá que les _____ (gustar).

5. Esperamos que Uds. _____ (tener) hambre.

6. Va a haber mucha comida. Quiero que Uds. la _____ (comer) toda.

7. Mis padres quieren que nosotros _____ (divertirse).

8. Pero ellos no quieren que nosotros _____ (hacer) mucho ruido.

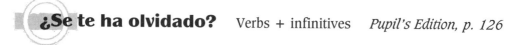 **¿Se te ha olvidado?**   Verbs + infinitives   *Pupil's Edition, p. 126*

Verbs like **querer** and **esperar** can be followed by **1)** an infinitive:
   Quiero ir a la playa.
or **2) que** and a verb in the subjunctive:
   Quiero que tú vengas conmigo a la playa.

Use **que** + subjunctive if there is more than one subject (**yo** and **tú**, for example).

The following verbs are often followed by a complementary infinitive:

deber	pensar	preferir	saber
esperar	poder	querer	tener que

---

9 Write each of the following sentences using complementary infinitives.

1. Mis hermanos y yo / querer / ir a la playa

_____

2. Primero / nosotros / tener que / preparar comida

_____

3. Mi hermano / preferir / ir a la playa del norte

_____

4. Mis otros amigos / pensar / buscar / a nosotros / allí

_____

5. Nosotros / esperar / pasar un buen rato

_____

6. Mi hermano Juan / poder / nadar bien

_____

HRW material copyrighted under notice appearing earlier in this work.

Sidebar: CAPÍTULO 5 Segundo paso

10 As you read Luis and Guadalupe's conversation, fill in the blanks with either the infinitive or the present subjunctive, as necessary.

GUADALUPE   Oye, Luis, ¿qué vas a **(1)** _____ (hacer) este verano?

LUIS   Bueno, mis padres quieren que yo **(2)** _____ (hacer) un

viaje para visitar a mis abuelos. Pero yo prefiero **(3)** _____ (quedarse) aquí para trabajar.

GUADALUPE   ¿Por qué no quieres **(4)** _____ (ir) a visitar a tus abuelos?

LUIS   No sé, muchas veces me aburro. Prefiero **(5)** _____ (trabajar) para ahorrar (*save*) dinero para la universidad.

GUADALUPE   ¿Piensas **(6)** _____ (asistir) a la universidad?

LUIS   Claro. Mis padres quieren que yo **(7)** _____ (estudiar) medicina.

GUADALUPE   De todas maneras, espero que tú lo **(8)** _____ (pasar) bien este verano.

11 Combine elements from each of the following boxes to write sentences.

yo		yo	ser amigo(s)
tú	querer	tú	hacer la tarea
mi mamá	esperar (que)	Juan	ir a la playa
nosotras		nosotros	ir al restaurante
Elena y Adolfo		María y Sabina	salir a comer
Claudia y Mariana		Sara y Martín	dar un paseo

1. _____

_____

2. _____

_____

3. _____

_____

4. _____

_____

5. _____

_____

6. _____

_____

Nota *Gramatical*   The subjunctive of **ir**   *Pupil's Edition, p. 127*

The verb **ir** is irregular in the present subjunctive.

que **vaya**	que **vayamos**
que **vayas**	que vayáis
que **vaya**	que **vayan**

12 Marcia and Simón are talking about where their parents want them to go to college. Fill in the blanks of their conversation with the correct subjunctive form of the verb **ir**.

MARCIA   Simón, ¿a qué universidad quieren tus padres que tú **(1)** _____ ?

SIMÓN   Bueno, quieren que yo **(2)** _____ a Buenos Aires para asistir a la Universidad Nacional.

MARCIA   ¿Te gustaría ir allí? Mis padres quieren que mi hermana y yo **(3)** _____ a Colombia.

SIMÓN   Pero queda tan lejos. Espero que Uds. no **(4)** _____ allí; de esa manera no podemos vernos.

MARCIA   Bueno, por lo menos, espero que **(5)** _____ mi hermana. Hace años que quiere ir allí.

13 Fill in the blanks with the correct form of **ir**. Use the infinitive or subjunctive, as necessary.

1. Queremos _____ al concierto después de cenar.

2. Esperamos que Gloria _____ con nosotros a la playa.

3. Ojalá que mis amigos _____ de compras conmigo.

4. Espero _____ a México para ver las pirámides.

5. ¿Quieres _____ al cine con nosotros esta noche?

6. Mateo quiere que nosotros _____ a comprar los ingredientes para el pastel.

7. Julia espera _____ en mi coche porque su coche no funciona.

14 Fill in the blanks of the following conversation with the appropriate forms of the verb **ir** (present indicative, preterite, present subjunctive, or infinitive).

BEN   ¿Quieres **(1)** _____ a la playa este fin de semana?

ANA   No sé. Mi novio quiere que nosotros **(2)** _____ al cine.

BEN   Pero Uds. **(3)** _____ al cine el fin de semana pasado.

ANA   Ya sé. Pero él quiere **(4)** _____ otra vez.

BEN   ¿Pero siempre tienes que **(5)** _____ adónde él quiere que

tú **(6)** _____ ?

ANA   Tienes razón. **(7)** _____ contigo. Él puede **(8)** _____ solo al cine.

CAPÍTULO 5 Segundo paso

Nota *G*ramatical   The subjuntive of **ser** and **dar**   *Pupil's Edition, p. 127*

- **Ser** and **dar** are irregular in the present subjunctive.
- The verb **dar** has an accent mark in the first and third person to distinguish it from the preposition **de**.

SER

que **sea**	que **seamos**
que **seas**	que séais
que **sea**	que **sean**

DAR

que **dé**	que **demos**
que **des**	que deis
que **dé**	que **den**

15 Fill in the following blanks with the correct present subjunctive form of **ser**.

1. Ayer fue horrible. Espero que hoy _____ mejor.

2. Hoy Maribel me va a presentar a su prima. Espero que _____ simpática.

3. Hoy tenemos dos exámenes. Ojalá que los dos no _____ difíciles.

4. Lo que nuestros padres quieren más es que mis hermanos y yo _____ felices.

5. Hoy tenemos un nuevo maestro. Espero que _____ amable.

16 Fill in the following blanks with the correct present subjunctive form of **dar**.

ELSA   ¿Qué quieres que tus padres te **(1)** _____ para tu cumpleaños?

DINO   Espero que me **(2)** _____ un coche, pero...

ELSA   ¿Qué quieres que Marta y yo te **(3)** _____ ?

DINO   No quiero que me **(4)** _____ nada. No es necesario.

ELSA   Bueno, si no quieres que te **(5)** _____ nada, no te lo daré.

17 Fill in the blanks with either the present indicative or present subjunctive of **ser** or **dar**.

CÉSAR   Oye, Emilio, ¿ **(1)** _____ difícil el profesor Pacheco?

EMILIO   Claro que sí. Siempre **(2)** _____ exámenes largos y difíciles.

CÉSAR   Tengo mi primer examen con él mañana. Espero que no

   (3) _____ difícil.

EMILIO   Si quieres que yo te **(4)** _____ un consejo, te recomiendo estudiar.

CÉSAR   Ojalá que el profesor nos **(5)** _____ buenos apuntes para estudiar.

EMILIO   Si quieres que yo te **(6)** _____ mis apuntes, llámame.

CÉSAR   Gracias. Estoy seguro que tus apuntes **(7)** _____ mejores que míos.

18 Fill in each of the following blanks with the correct form of **ser** or **dar** (present indicative, preterite, present subjunctive, or infinitive).

Esta noche va a (1) _____ muy divertida porque la voy a pasar con mi

novio, Andrés. Él (2) _____ muy amable; su mamá quiere prepararme una

cena especial. Ojalá que la cena (3) _____ buena. Él no sabe cocinar bien.

La vez pasada, él vino a mi casa y fuimos a (4) _____ un paseo al parque.

Espero que (5) _____ un paseo por el parque esta noche también. Es que

cada vez que (6) _____ un paseo, lo pasamos bien. (7) _____

muy románticos los paseos por el parque. Ojalá que él y yo (8) _____ novios

por mucho tiempo. (9) _____ muy compatibles.

19 Complete each of the following sentences with a logical wish or hope using the cues in parentheses. Begin each sentence with **ojalá que**, **esperar que**, or **querer que**.

MODELO   Está muy nublado hoy. (no llover)
         Ojalá que no llueva.

1. Voy a hacer una fiesta esta noche. (mis amigos venir)

   _____

2. Juan va a traer la música. (la música ser buena)

   _____

3. Vamos a servir mucha comida. (mis amigos tener hambre)

   _____

4. Mis amigos van a traer regalos. (ellos darme muchos)

   _____

5. Mis padres no me han dicho qué van a darme. (darme un carro)

   _____

6. Mi hermana me ha dicho que me va a dar un disco compacto. (ser de "Deep Blue Something").

   _____

7. No sé qué me van a dar mis abuelos. (ser dinero)

   _____

8. No sé qué sabor de helado tienen. (ser de chocolate)

   _____

CAPÍTULO 5 Segundo paso

El arte y la música

PRIMER PASO

To introduce and change a topic of conversation, you'll need to use some expressions. To express what needs to be done, you'll need to use the subjunctive after expressions of need.

VOCABULARIO   El arte   *Pupil's Edition, p. 143*

1 For each set of words, choose the word that doesn't belong and write it in the space provided.

_____ 1. el escultor   la cantante   el artista   la orquesta

_____ 2. la danza   la escultura   la pintura   la estatua

_____ 3. contemporáneo   antiguo   moderno   nuevo

_____ 4. el dibujo   la pintura   la escultora   la escultura

_____ 5. la orquesta   el bailarín   el músico   el cantante

_____ 6. diseñar   tocar   pintar   aprender

_____ 7. la estatua   la bailarina   la pintura   el concierto

2 For each description, write the name of the artistic profession in the space provided.

> los bailarines   el músico   el escultor   la escultora
> la cantante   los artistas   la artista   la bailarina

_____ 1. A Mario le encanta hacer esculturas. Las hace muy bien.

_____ 2. Sergio toca muy bien el piano. Toca en la Orquesta Municipal.

_____ 3. Gloria y Federico están locos por la danza, sobre todo bailes folclóricos.

_____ 4. Silvia es aficionada de la pintura. Le gusta pintar.

_____ 5. Catarina canta mejor que todos los estudiantes de la escuela.

_____ 6. Mercedes es experta en hacer estatuas de gente y animales.

_____ 7. Elisa y Juan Pablo son muy creativos. Tienen una exhibición de su cerámica en la biblioteca.

3 Fill in the blanks in the following paragraph with an appropriate word from the box.

pinturas	bailarines	antiguo	orquesta	intentar	dibujo
músico	esculturas	exhibiciones	diseñar	patrocinar	conciertos

La Fundación Artística va a **(1)** _____ la construcción de un centro de

arte muy grande. El centro va a tener mucho espacio para las **(2)** _____

de todo tipo de **(3)** _____ y **(4)** _____ . También va a

tener un auditorio para la música. Nuestra **(5)** _____ cívica ya tiene

planes para dar muchos **(6)** _____ allí. Van a **(7)** _____
dar por lo menos un concierto cada mes. Y además La Organización de la Danza

Folklórica quiere comenzar un programa para los **(8)** _____ jóvenes.
Y por fin, el departamento de arte piensa usar el centro para dar cursos de

(9) _____ .

Nota Gramatical   Gender of nouns   *Pupil's Edition, p. 143*

- Nouns ending in -**o** are usually masculine (**el carro**) and nouns ending in -**a** are usually feminine (**la puerta**).
- Nouns ending in -**e** or a consonant may be either masculine (**el baile**) or feminine (**la clase**).
- Nouns that end in -**ista** refer to people and may be either masculine or feminine depending on the actual gender of the person they refer to (**el periodista, la artista**). The article used indicates the gender.
- Some words ending -**o** may refer to a female (**la modelo**).

4 In each of the following sentences, write the word that best completes the sentence.

1. Nos gusta mucho ir a escuchar un _____ (concierto / orquesta).

2. Las _____ (exhibiciones / pintura) del Museo de Arte son muy buenas.

3. En nuestra _____ (país / sociedad) hay muchos _____
   (pinturas / artistas) famosos.

4. Esa _____ (estatua / dibujo) es muy famosa. Claudia Obregón fue la

   _____ (modelo / escultor).

5. Es posible ir al parque para ver las _____ (estatuas / dibujos) durante el

   _____ (noche / día).

¡Ven conmigo! Level 3, Chapter 6

Grammar and Vocabulary Workbook **47**

HRW material copyrighted under notice appearing earlier in this work.

CAPÍTULO 6 Primer paso

Nota *G*ramatical   The subjunctive of **hacer**   *Pupil's Edition, p. 144*

- The subjunctive mood occurs after expressions like **hace falta que, es necesario que, es importante que,** and other expressions that talk about the need for something to happen.

  Es necesario que <u>hagas</u> ejercicio.
  Hace falta que <u>hagamos</u> la tarea todos los días.

- The verb **hacer** is irregular in the subjunctive.

que	**haga**	que	**hagamos**
que	**hagas**	que	hagáis
que	**haga**	que	**hagan**

5 Fill in the blanks with the correct form of the present subjunctive of **hacer**.

SOFÍA   Marcos, ¿qué quieres que yo (1) _____ para la fiesta?

MARCOS   Bueno, hace falta que nosotros (2) _____ los refrescos.

SOFÍA   ¿Quieres que yo los (3) _____ ?

MARCOS   No, es necesario que tú (4) _____ las decoraciones. Tú eres más creativa.

SOFÍA   Entonces, ¿quién va a hacer la comida?

MARCOS   Espero que mis padres la (5) _____ .

6 Fill in the blanks in the following sentences with the correct form of the present indicative, the present subjunctive, or the infinitive of **hacer**.

El arte y la música son muy populares en nuestra

sociedad. Todos podemos (1) _____

algo para patrocinarlos. Por ejemplo, en mi familia

nosotros (2) _____ mucho: vamos a los

conciertos y damos dinero a los museos. Mis padres

dicen que es muy importante que nosotros

(3) _____ algo. Quiero que mis amigos

(4) _____ algo también, pero no

les interesa. Ellos no (5) _____ nada.

Hace falta que todos (6) _____ una

contribución al arte.

CAPÍTULO 6 Primer paso

7 For each of the following problems, write a possible solution.

    MODELO   Saqué una mala nota en el examen. (tú / estudiar más)
        Es necesario que estudies más.

  1. Nuestra orquesta toca muy mal. (ellos / practicar)

_____

_____

  2. No hay nada de arte en nuestro colegio. (nosotros / poner)

_____

_____

  3. Mis hermanos no saben nada de la literatura. (ellos / leer más)

_____

_____

  4. Nuestro concierto es mañana y todavía no estamos listos. (nosotros / prepararse)

_____

_____

  5. El público tiene sed durante el concierto. (nosotros / servirles refrescos)

_____

_____

¿Te acuerdas? Infinitives after impersonal expressions   *Pupil's Edition, p. 144*

After expressions like **hace falta**, **es necesario**, **es importante**, and other expressions that talk about the need for something to happen, use an infinitive if it needs to be done in general by everyone and not a specific person:

    Es necesario **comer** bien.

---

8 For each phrase, write a sentence saying what needs to be done in general by everyone.

    MODELO   Todo el mundo está agobiado. (descansar)   **Es importante descansar.**

  1. No hay dinero para las artes. (patrocinar las artes)

_____

  2. Nunca ha habido una exhibición en nuestra ciudad. (invitar a un artista)

_____

  3. No se puede escuchar música en vivo (*live*) en nuestra ciudad. (formar una orquesta)

_____

CAPÍTULO 6 Primer paso

VOCABULARIO   Opiniones   *Pupil's Edition, p. 145*

9 Choose the word that best summarizes the description and write it in the space provided.

maravillosas   originales   incomprensibles

magnífico   insoportable   pésima

_____ 1. Me encanta este cuadro. Es el mejor cuadro del mundo.

_____ 2. Encuentro genial las pinturas de Frida Kahlo.

_____ 3. Mi prima Sara molesta mucho. No hay quien la aguante.

_____ 4. Las esculturas que están en el museo ahora me dejan frío.

_____ 5. Admiro mucho las novelas de Isabel Allende. Son buenas.

_____ 6. Me cae gordo la música de Maná. Es la peor música del mundo.

¿Se te ha olvidado?   Comparisons   *Pupil's Edition, p. 146*

10 An art critic has compiled the following notes on the new exhibit at the museum. Use the ratings to write sentences comparing the work of the artists listed below. A rating of "5" is the highest.

	"Uno" de Solar	"National Holiday" de Botero	"La Huida" de Varo	"Las Meninas" de Velásquez
original	5	5	4	4
realista	1	3	4	5
creativo	3	5	5	4
imaginativo	2	2	4	5

MODELO   <u>"Uno" de Solar es tan original como "National Holiday" de Botero.</u>

1. Botero / Solar / original

_____

2. Varo / Botero / creativo

_____

3. Solar / Velásquez / imaginativo

_____

4. Varo / Velásquez / realista

_____

5. Botero / Velásquez / creativo

_____

■ SEGUNDO PASO

To make suggestions and recommendations, you may want to use the present subjunctive. To turn down an invitation, you may need to use **nosotros** commands.

ASÍ SE DICE   Making suggestions   *Pupil's Edition, p. 150*
and recommendations

11 Make a suggestion for each of the following comments using the present subjunctive after a recommendation.

MODELO   Estoy cansado. (yo / aconsejar / tú / descansar)
Te aconsejo que descanses.

1. Tengo frío. (yo / sugerir / tú / ponerse un suéter)

   _____

   _____

2. Mis padres están agobiados. (nosotros / recomendar / ellos / tomar las cosas con calma)

   _____

   _____

3. Mi clase de química es muy difícil. (mi profesora / aconsejar / yo / estudiar más)

   _____

   _____

4. La exhibición de Botero está en nuestra ciudad. (mis amigos / recomendar / yo / verla)

   _____

   _____

5. La música de Mecano la encuentro genial. (yo / recomendar / tú / comprar su nuevo disco)

   _____

   _____

6. Perla quiere ir al concierto de la orquesta. (nosotros / sugerir / ella / comprar los boletos pronto)

   _____

   _____

7. Daniel y Norma piensan ser artistas. (es mejor / ellos / estudiar en un instituto de arte)

   _____

   _____

HRW material copyrighted under notice appearing earlier in this work.

CAPÍTULO 6 Segundo paso

¿Te acuerdas? Irregular subjunctives *Pupil's Edition, p. 150*

Ser, **ir**, and **dar** are irregular in the present subjunctive.

SER		IR		DAR	
sea	seamos	vaya	vayamos	dé	demos
seas	seáis	vayas	vayáis	des	deis
sea	sean	vaya	vayan	dé	den

---

12 Fill in each of the following sentences with the correct present subjunctive form or **ser**, **ir**, or **dar**.

1. ¿Adónde quieren Uds. que nosotros _____ este verano?

2. Las vacaciones del año pasado fueron horribles. Espero que las de este verano

   _____ mejores.

3. Mi amiga Juana recomienda que yo _____ al Caribe.

4. Pero mi amigo Marcos dice que es mejor que nosotros _____ a Europa.

5. Marisol recomienda que Uds. _____ un paseo por el Yunque si van a
   Puerto Rico.

6. Pero si tú vas a Europa, te aconsejo que _____ un paseo por el Parque
   del Retiro.

7. No sé adónde vamos, pero ojalá que el lugar _____ bonito.

13 Fill in the conversation with either the present indicative, the present subjunctive, or the infinitve of **ser**, **ir**, or **dar**.

MARIANA   Hola, Vivian. Tú sabes que mañana es el cumpleaños de Ricardo. ¿Qué quieres que

nosotras le **(1)** _____ ?

VIVIAN   Bueno, creo que él quiere que sus padres le **(2)** _____ un estéreo.

Entonces, yo recomiendo que nosotras le **(3)** _____ un disco
compacto.

MARIANA   Entonces, sugiero que nosotras **(4)** _____ a hacer compras al
centro comercial.

VIVIAN   Buena idea. A propósito, mi papá me aconseja que yo **(5)** _____

temprano porque luego quiere que la familia **(6)** _____ a cenar a la
casa de mis abuelos.

MARIANA   Muy bien. Ojalá que **(7)** _____ fácil encontrar algo para Marcos.

14 Sra. Sábelotodo, a local advice columnist, is advising Severiano on how to get along better with his girlfriend. Combine elements from each of the following boxes to create her recommendations and suggestions for Severiano.

| aconsejar |
| recomendar |
| sugerir |

| tú |
| Uds. |

| hablarle más | salir más |
| no pelear | tomar las cosas con calma |

1. _____

2. _____

3. _____

4. _____

*G*ramática   **Nosotros** commands   *Pupil's Edition, p. 152*

• To say "Let's", use **vamos a** + infinitive or use the **nosotros** form of the present subjunctive:

¡**Vamos a ver** una película!   ¡**Veamos** una película!

• To say "Let's not," use **no** + the **nosotros** form of the present subjunctive:

¡**No veamos** una película!

• Use ¡**Vamos!** to say "Let's go!"

• Attach any pronouns to the end of an affirmative command and place them before a negative command:

¡Hagámos**lo** mañana!   ¡No **lo** hagamos hoy!

15 For each of the following statements, write one command urging your friends to do something and one urging them not to do something.

1. Estamos aburridos. (no quedarse en casa / ir al parque)

_____

_____

2. Tenemos hambre. (no comer en casa / hacer un picnic)

_____

_____

3. Hay un examen mañana. (no salir / estudiar)

_____

_____

4. El cumpleaños de Rosana es mañana. (hacerle una fiesta / no decírselo)

_____

_____

CAPÍTULO 6 Segundo paso

Nota *G*ramatical   Commands   *Pupil's Edition, p. 152*

To form the **nosotros** commands, add **-mos** to the Ud. command form.

hable	→	hablemos
traiga	→	traigamos

16 For each of the following invitations, write a refusal saying "Let's not..." Then offer to reschedule by saying "Let's..."

MODELO   ¿Quieres ir al parque?   **No vayamos hoy. Vamos mañana.**

1. ¿Te gustaría ver la exhibición en el museo?

_____

_____

2. ¿Quieres tomar un café esta tarde?

_____

_____

3. ¿Qué tal si vamos de compras?

_____

_____

4. ¿Te gustaría dar un paseo en el parque?

_____

_____

17 You and all your friends are putting together a surprise party for Adela. Your friend Mateo tends to order everyone around without offering to help. For each of the following commands that he gives, make it a **nosotros** command to convince him to help.

MODELO   ¡Limpien la sala!   **¡Limpiémosla todos!**

1. Decoren Uds. la sala.

_____

2. Manden Uds. las invitaciones.

_____

3. Pongan Uds. los refrescos en la mesa.

_____

4. Llamen Uds. a los invitados.

_____

5. No le digan nada a Adela.

_____

CAPÍTULO 7 — Dime con quién andas

■ PRIMER PASO

When expressing happiness and unhappiness, you'll need to use the subjunctive.

> **Gramática** The subjunctive with expressions of feelings — *Pupil's Edition, p. 172*
>
> When expressing an emotional reaction to something, the emotional reaction is in the indicative mood and the event being reacted to is in the subjunctive mood:
>
> El maestro **se alegra que** sus estudiantes **hagan la tarea** todos los días.

1 Write the correct present subjunctive form of the verb in parentheses.

1. Me alegro que Uds. _____ (poder) venir conmigo a la playa.

2. Ojalá que no _____ (llover).

3. Temo que Silvia no _____ (venir) porque tiene que trabajar.

4. Sentimos que Silvia _____ (tener) que trabajar hoy.

5. Pero nos alegramos que hoy _____ (hacer) buen tiempo.

6. Me frustra que mis amigos _____ (trabajar) en vez de divertirse.

7. Silvia siente que nosotras _____ (pasar) un día en la playa sin ella.

2 Write your emotional reactions to each of the following situations. Use expressions like **me alegro que** and **siento que** plus the subjunctive.

1. Mis profesores son amables.

   _____

2. Los estudiantes sacan mejores notas este semestre.

   _____

3. Mi mejor amigo va a otro colegio.

   _____

4. Mis abuelos no vienen a visitarnos.

   _____

5. La comida de la cafetería es muy mala.

   _____

¿Te acuerdas? Complementary infinitives *Pupil's Edition, p. 172*

3 Complete the paragraph with the present indicative, present subjunctive, or the infinitive.

Espero que este año escolar **(1)** _____ (ser) muy divertido. Parece que

yo **(2)** _____ (tener) muchas clases con mi amigo Pablo. Estoy contenta

de **(3)** _____ (estar) en clase con él. Es un buen amigo. Espero que mi

novio Rafa no **(4)** _____ (estar) enojado por eso. A él no le gusta que

Pablo y yo **(5)** _____ (ser) amigos. Me duele mucho que no le

(6) _____ (gustar). Pablo y yo nos **(7)** _____ (conocer)

desde hace mucho tiempo y nosotros **(8)** _____ (tener) mucho en común.

¿Se te ha olvidado? Irregular subjunctives *Pupil's Edition, pp. 336–356*

4 Fill in the blanks with the correct present subjunctive forms of the verbs in parentheses.

1. Mamá y papá quieren que tú y yo _____ (ir) al parque.

2. Ellos recomiendan que yo _____ (dar) un paseo porque hace sol.

3. Me alegro que mis padres _____ (ser) muy amables.

4. Ojalá que _____ (haber) algo interesante en el parque.

5. Temo que mis amigos no _____ (estar) allí.

5 Fill in each blank with the present indicative or subjunctive of an appropriate verb from the box.

ir	estar	dar	haber	ser

MARCOS   Emilia, Carlos me dice que tú **(1)**_____ enojada conmigo.

EMILIA   Estoy enojada que tú nunca **(2)** _____ conmigo a los bailes.

MARCOS   Pero, tú sabes que tengo que trabajar todos los fines de semana. No tengo tiempo.

EMILIA   Todas mis amigas creen que tienes otra novia.

MARCOS   Bueno, yo **(3)** _____ seguro que tú no te lo crees. Me duele

mucho que tus amigas **(4)** _____ tan chismosas.

EMILIA   Me alegro que el rumor no **(5)** _____ verdad.

MARCOS   A ver , . . . espero que **(6)** _____ algo que podamos hacer para
resolver el problema.

EMILIA   ¿Qué tal si nosotros **(7)** _____ un paseo por el parque para hablar?

VOCABULARIO   La amistad y el amor   *Pupil's Edition, p. 173*

6 Match each situation on the left with the sentence on the right that summarizes it.

_____ 1. Carolina y yo hemos sido amigas por muchos años.

_____ 2. Esperé por dos horas pero Carlos nunca llegó.

_____ 3. Yo no quiero hablarle a Ramón ni él a mí.

_____ 4. Siempre me dicen que me veo muy guapo.

_____ 5. Paco y yo hemos tenido un malentendido.

a. Han dejado de hablarse.

b. Le hacen un cumplido.

c. Tienen una buena amistad.

d. Ella creía que iba con él al baile, pero él no quería.

e. La dejó plantada.

7 Patricia wrote a letter to a local advice columnist. Read the letter and fill in the blanks with an appropriate word from the box. Conjugate the verbs as necessary and make sure all adjectives agree.

> apoyar   reconciliarse   contar   tener un malentendido
>
> decepcionado   rumor   dejar plantado

Yo siempre (1) _____ mucho con mi amiga Debra y siempre nos hemos apoyado. Pero estoy muy (2) _____ . Algunas amigas mías me dijeron que ella chismeaba de mí. Ella me vio en el cine hace unos días. Yo esperaba a Rafael. Ella pensó que él me (3) _____ y comenzó un (4) _____ que él y yo nos peleamos. Yo confiaba en Debra, pero no la puedo perdonar. Ella y yo hemos dejado de hablarnos y no sé si quiero que nosotras (5) _____ .

8 How would the advice columnist express the following advice in Spanish?

1. I'm sorry you and Debra aren't speaking.

_____

2. It seems you've had a misunderstanding.

_____

3. I recommend that you make up.

_____

4. I hope you (pl.) solve the problem.

_____

Nota *G*ramatical   Reciprocal actions   *Pupil's Edition, p. 173*

- To express *each other* use a plural reflexive form of the verb:

  Mitch y Trisha **se quieren** mucho.   Tú y yo **nos hablamos** a menudo.

- In Spanish, *each other* is always stated using the reflexive pronoun:

  Juan y María no **se hablan**.   *John and Mary aren't speaking (to each other).*

9 Clara is describing what happened between Patricia and Mauricio. How would she rephrase the following situations using reflexive pronouns?

1. Hubo un malentendido entre Patricia y Mauricio ayer.

   _____

2. Hoy él no le habla a ella y ella no le habla a él tampoco.

   _____

3. Espero que hagan las paces.

   _____

4. Ella lo quiere mucho a él y él la quiere mucho a ella.

   _____

*G*ramática   The present perfect subjunctive   *Pupil's Edition, p. 174*

- The present perfect subjunctive is the present subjunctive of **haber** (**haya**, **hayas**, **haya**, **hayamos**, hayáis, **hayan**) and the past participle of a verb (-**ado**, -**ido**).

- To express an emotional reaction to something that has already happened, state the emotional reaction in the present indicative and the event that has happened in the present perfect subjunctive:

  El maestro **se alegra que** todos los estudiantes **hayan hecho** su tarea.

- To express a hope that something has already happened, state the hope in the present indicative and the event in the present perfect subjunctive.

  El maestro **espera que** todos **hayan salido** bien en el examen.

10 Complete each sentence with the present perfect subjunctive of the verb in parentheses.

1. Silvia espera que su novio le _____ (comprar) algo para su cumpleaños.

2. Mis padres están contentos que yo _____ (sacar) buenas notas.

3. Me sorprende mucho que Sara y Miguel _____ (pelearse).

4. Me alegro que tú _____ (confiar) en mí por tantos años.

5. El profesor espera que los estudiantes no _____ (tener) un malentendido.

11 How would the people in parentheses react to the following situations? Use the present perfect subjunctive.

MODELO   Francisca dejó de hablarle a su novio Martín. (Martín / estar triste)
Martín está triste que Francisca haya dejado de hablarle.

1. Mis padres no me permitieron salir este viernes. (yo / estar triste)

_____

_____

2. Carlota y yo nos peleamos. (Carlota / sentir)

_____

_____

3. Saqué una buena nota en el examen de álgebra. (mi profesora / alegrarse)

_____

_____

4. Decidí asisitir a la universidad después de graduarme. (mis padres / estar contento)

_____

_____

5. Pusiste la mesa para la cena. (tu mamá / estar contento)

_____

_____

12 Use the following cues to write what each person hopes has or hasn't happened. Use a form of **esperar que**.

MODELO   Está lloviendo. (yo / tú / traer un paraguas)
Espero que hayas traído un paraguas.

1. Selina se ve muy decepcionada. (yo / ella / salir bien en el examen)

_____

_____

2. ¡Vamos a invitar a Josefina a cenar! (nosotros / ella / no comer todavía)

_____

_____

3. Gerardo no ha llegado todavía. (sus amigos / a él / no acabársele la gasolina)

_____

_____

4. Parece que hay muchos recados en el contestador. (yo / mi novio / llamar)

_____

_____

■ SEGUNDO PASO

To make an apology, you'll need some specific vocabulary. You might also use affirmative and negative words and the subjunctive to indicate what is unknown or nonexistent.

VOCABULARIO Problemas y soluciones *Pupil's Edition, p. 179*

13 Roberto isn't on good terms with his brother Ignacio. Read each situation on the left and match it with a sentence that summarizes it. Some situations will have more than one summary.

_____ 1. Roberto quedó ofendido porque su hermano Ignacio salió con su novia Raquel.

_____ 2. Ahora Roberto y Raquel ya no son novios.

_____ 3. Roberto no quiere decirle ni una palabra a su hermano.

_____ 4. Raquel quiere que Roberto la perdone.

a. Roberto y su hermano han dejado de hablarse.

b. Raquel ha admitido su error.

c. Roberto rompió con Raquel.

d. Ignacio insultó a Roberto.

e. Roberto tiene celos de su hermano Ignacio.

f. Roberto y Ignacio no han discutido el problema.

14 Roberto wrote a letter to an advice column about the situation with Ignacio and Raquel. Fill in the response he got with an appropriate word or phrase from the box.

admitirán   celos   te das tiempo   hayas roto   desleales

le compras un regalo   discutas el problema   insultaste

Hola Roberto, siento mucho que

(1) _____ con tu novia. Pero, es

muy importante que (2) _____ con

ella. Estoy seguro que Ignacio y Raquel

(3) _____ su error. Si

(4) _____ para pensar, vas a poder

perdonarlos. No tengas (5) _____.

No tengo la impresión de que ellos sean

(6) _____ ¡Buena suerte!

*G*ramática Affirmative, indefinite, *Pupil's Edition, p. 181*
and negative words

algo *something*	**nada** *nothing*
alguien *someone, anyone*	**nadie** *nobody, no one*
algún, alguno(a) *some, any*	**ningún, ninguno**(a) *no, none*
siempre *always*	**nunca** *never*

• When two or more negative words are used, **no** comes before the verb:

No quiere venir **nunca**.   **No** quiere venir **nadie**.

• If **no** comes first, the next indefinite word must be negative:

¿Hay **alguien** en el baño?   **No, no** hay **nadie** en el baño.

¿Quieres **algo**?   **No, no** quiero **nada**.

15 Fill in the blanks in the following conversation with an appropriate affirmative or negative word. Use the cues in parentheses.

MANOLO   Oye, Teresa, ¿quieres venir a comer **(1)** _____ *(something)?*

TERESA   Sí, claro, pero ¿por qué no invitamos a **(2)** _____ *(someone)* más? Cuanto más gente, mejor, ¿no?

MANOLO   Bueno, ya he invitado a tres personas y **(3)** _____ *(no one)*

puede venir. Pero sabía que podía contar contigo. Tú **(4)** _____ *(always)* quieres ir conmigo.

TERESA   Tú sabes que **(5)** _____ *(never)* te puedo decir "no." ¿Nos vamos?

MANOLO   Espérate, tengo que hacer **(6)** _____ *(some)* cosas antes.

TERESA   ¿Tienes que hacerlas ahora mismo? Tengo hambre.

MANOLO   Bueno, no es **(7)** _____ *(nothing)* importante. ¡Vamos!

16 Armando is a very negative person. For each of the following answers that he's given, write what the question probably was.

1. — _____
— No, no quiero nada para beber.

2. — _____
— No, no conozco a nadie de España.

3. — _____
— No, no falto a clase casi nunca.

4. — _____
— No, no hay nada para comer.

5. — _____
— No, no tengo ninguna idea por qué dices que soy negativo.

*G*ramática   The subjunctive with the unknown   *Pupil's Edition, p. 181*
or nonexistent

- When referring back to something or someone unknown, indefinite, or nonexistent, use **que** + the subjunctive:

    Quiero comer un postre **que no tenga** muchas calorías.

    No existe ningún postre **que no tenga** muchas calorías.

- When referring back to something or someone definite, use the indicative:

    Pues, hay muchos postres que no **tienen** muchas calorías. ¿Cuál prefieres?

- The subjunctive is only necessary when referring back to the indefinite or nonexistent with **que**, not when the indefinite word is the subject of the sentence:

    Aquí nadie **habla** inglés.

17 Fill in the blanks in the following conversation with either the present indicative or the present subjunctive of the verb in parentheses.

SR. PEÑA   No me gusta. ¿No tienen una que **(1)** _____ (ser) de seda?

SRA. LADO   Lo siento, señor. Nosotros no **(2)** _____ (tener) ninguna

camisa que **(3)** _____ (ser) de seda.

SR. PEÑA   ¡Qué lástima! ¿Sabe Ud. si hay otra tienda que **(4)** _____ (vender) camisas de seda?

SRA. LADO   Sí, hay una tienda en la Avenida 7 que sí las **(5)** _____ (tener).

SR. PEÑA   ¿Hay un autobús que me **(6)** _____ (poder) llevar a la Avenida 7?

SRA. LADO   Sí, Ud. puede ir en el número 12. Ese autobús **(7)** _____ (ir) directamente a la tienda.

18 Mario and Susana are doing their grocery shopping. Fill in their conversation with either the present subjunctive or present indicative of the verb in parentheses.

SUSANA   Oye, Mario, ¿qué clase de refresco **(1)** _____ (querer) tú?

MARIO   Quiero uno que **(2)** _____ (tener) sabor a fruta.

SUSANA   ¿Qué te parece si nosotros **(3)** _____ (comprar) Colazucarona?

MARIO   Ese refresco **(4)** _____ (llevar) mucho azúcar, ¿no?

SUSANA   Tienes razón. Pero hay otros que **(5)** _____ (ser) menos dulces.

MARIO   Sí, voy a comprar Colalayte, que no **(6)** _____ (ser) muy dulce. ¿Qué quieres tomar tú?

SUSANA   Quiero un refresco que no **(7)** _____ (costar) mucho porque no tengo mucho dinero hoy.

19 Alberto needs to make a few changes in his life. Use the cues below to write what Alberto needs to do.

MODELO   Alberto nunca lleva esa camisa porque es muy grande. (necesitar / quedarle bien)
Alberto necesita una camisa que le quede bien.

1. El diccionario de Alberto no tiene buenas traducciones. (deber / buscar / tener mejores traducciones)

_____

_____

2. El coche de Alberto no funciona bien. (querer / comprar / funcionar mejor)

_____

_____

3. La cámara de Alberto ya no sirve bien. (deber / comprar / servir mejor)

_____

_____

4. El regalo que compró para su novia es de mala calidad. (deber / encontrar / ser de mejor calidad)

_____

_____

5. Su clase de química es muy difícil. (deber / tomar / ser más fácil)

_____

_____

20 Hortensia has gone to her counselor because she's having trouble making friends. Use the following notes to write the counselor's report. Use the present indicative or subjunctive as necessary.

1. Hortensia / buscar / amigo / que / apoyarla

_____

2. también / ella / necesitar / amigo / que / respetar sus sentimientos

_____

3. ella / no conocer / nadie / que / ser leal

_____

4. al pelearse / ninguno de sus amigos / admitir su error

_____

5. ella / decir que / nadie / conocerla bien

_____

CAPÍTULO 8

Los medios de comunicación

■ PRIMER PASO

To express doubt and disbelief, you'll need to use certain expressions and the subjunctive mood. To express certainty, you'll need to use specific vocabulary and expressions.

Nota Gramatical Subjunctive after expressions *Pupil's Edition, p. 197* of doubt

After **dudar**, **no creer**, and other expressions of doubt or disbelief, use **que** plus a verb in the subjunctive mood.

No creo que la biología **sea** más difícil que las matemáticas.

---

1 Complete these sentences with the correct present subjunctive form of an appropriate verb.

| *necesitar* | *quedarse* | *haber* | *poder* | *ser* | *tener* |

1. Es imposible que _____ 19 emisoras en nuestra ciudad.

2. Parece mentira que el cable _____ llevar hasta 100 canales.

3. Dudo que nosotros _____ tantos canales.

4. Tampoco creo que todas las emisoras _____ buenos programas.

5. No creo que una persona _____ frente a la tele para ver los programas.

2 Respond to these statements with an expression of doubt, like **dudo que** and **no creo que**.

MODELO   El mundo es pequeño.   **No creo que el mundo sea pequeño.**

1. La clase de francés es más interesante que la clase de español.

_____

2. La comida mexicana se prepara con menos salsa picante que la comida italiana.

_____

3. Los estadounidenses manejan sus coches menos que los españoles.

_____

4. El planeta Júpiter es más pequeño que la Tierra.

_____

5. Rhode Island es más grande que Alaska.

_____

3 Fill in the conversation between Alba and Esteban with either the present indicative or present subjunctive of the verb in parentheses.

ALBA   Oye, Esteban, ¿crees que todo lo que hay en los periódicos

(1) _____ (ser) verdad?

ESTEBAN   No sé. Creo que la prensa (2) _____ (tener) la responsabilidad de

escribir la verdad, pero es posible que (3) _____ (haber) errores.

ALBA   Sí. Por ejemplo, aquí hay un anuncio en el periódico que

(4) _____ (decir) que el presidente visita Australia. Pero yo sé

que el presidente (5) _____ (estar) hoy en Salzburg, Austria.

ESTEBAN   Sí, eso tiene que ser un error. Dudo que (6) _____ (ser) posible

que (7) _____ (existir) un periódico perfecto.

VOCABULARIO   La televisión   *Pupil's Edition, p. 198*

4 Choose the word from the word box that matches each description and write it in the blank provided.

> anunciar   la cadena   el locutor
>
>   el reportaje
>
> el canal   la prensa   el documental

_____ 1. El programa de televisión que nos enseña algo de las ciencias, la historia u otra cosa educativa.

_____ 2. La persona que nos habla en el noticiero.

_____ 3. La compañía que produce los programas de televisión o de radio.

_____ 4. La organización que se hace responsable de las noticias del mundo.

_____ 5. El número que se usa para sintonizar *(tune in)* una emisora.

5 For each of the following groups of words, choose the word that doesn't belong and write it in the space provided.

_____ 1. la emisora   el canal   la prensa   la cadena

_____ 2. el programa   el anuncio   el reportaje   el documental

_____ 3. el documental   el comentarista   el locutor   la locutora

_____ 4. el canal   la emisora   la cadena   el comentarista

_____ 5. el documental   el reportaje   el noticiero   la emisora

_____ 6. la radio   la televisión   la prensa   el programa

ASÍ SE DICE   Expressing certainty   *Pupil's Edition, p. 199*

6 Fill in each of the following blanks with an expression of doubt or certainty as required by the context. Use expressions from the box.

no puedo creer	todo el mundo sabe	es obvio
estoy convencida	duda	
	por cierto	está seguro

1. _____ que los anuncios de los periódicos siempre digan la verdad.

2. _____ que muchas veces los periódicos tienen errores.

3. Juan _____ que haya un documental en la televisión esta noche.

4. _____ que el noticiero es una buena manera de mantenerse al tanto.

5. Mi papá _____ que esta cadena sólo tiene programas infantiles.

6. _____ que México queda al sur de los Estados Unidos.

VOCABULARIO   Saber y no saber   *Pupil's Edition, p. 200*

7 Fill in the conversation with an appropriate expression from the box.

¿Qué sé yo?	Que yo sepa	jota
la menor idea	Ya lo sé	a chino	al tanto de

SEVERIANO ¿Has oído que el presidente va a visitar nuestra ciudad?

BEATRIZ (1) _____. Lo leí esta mañana en el periódico.

SEVERIANO ¿Siempre lees el periódico?

BEATRIZ Sí. Creo que es muy importante estar (2) _____ las noticias. ¿Tú lees siempre el periódico?

SEVERIANO No, nunca. Por eso no tengo (3) _____ de lo que está pasando. ¿Por cuánto tiempo va a quedarse el presidente?

BEATRIZ (4)_____, piensa quedarse nada más por dos días. ¿Quieres venir conmigo a oírle hablar?

SEVERIANO No, gracias, no sé ni (5) _____ de la política. Los discursos políticos me suenan (6) _____.

¿Se te ha olvidado?   Uses of se   *Pupil's Edition, p. 336-356*

The word **se** can be used:

1. as a reflexive pronoun   Juan **se** levanta a las 6.
2. as an indirect object pronoun in   ¿Las llaves? **Se** las di a María.
   combination with **lo**, **la**, **los**, **las**
3. as an indefinite subject like *you*, *one*,   En esta clase **se** trabaja mucho.
   or *they*

8 Answer each of the following questions using the cues in parentheses. Use direct and indirect object pronouns in your answers. Conjugate all verbs in the preterite tense.

1. ¿Qué hiciste con el periódico, Carlos? (yo / dar / a mamá)

   _____

2. Mamá, ¿sabes quién tiene las tiras cómicas? (yo / dar / a Sandra)

   _____

3. ¿Quién te dio esa revista, Jabi? (Alba / dar / a mí)

   _____

4. Alba, ¿quién te dio esa revista? (mi profesor / prestar / a mí)

   _____

5. ¿Quién te dijo las noticias, Esteban? (Paulina / decir / a nosotros)

   _____

6. ¿Y a quién le dijiste las noticias tú? (yo / decir / a todos mis amigos)

   _____

9 Rewrite each of the following sentences, replacing any indefinite subjects with **se**.

1. Es necesario que todos lean el periódico todos los días.

   _____

2. No creo que uno necesite mucho tiempo para leerlo.

   _____

3. Es increíble que uno no esté bien informado.

   _____

4. La gente duda que haya tiempo para ponerse al tanto de las noticias.

   _____

5. Que yo sepa, todos creen que es fácil leer.

   _____

■ SEGUNDO PASO

To express possibility and impossibility, you'll need to use the subjunctive mood after impersonal expressions. To express surprise, you'll need to know various expressions.

*G*ramática Subjunctive after impersonal expressions *Pupil's Edition, p. 204*

• Impersonal expressions of doubt, denial, surprise, emotion, or other personal judgment are usually followed by the subjunctive:

Es dudoso que
Es sorprendiente que
Es importante que } ella **llegue** a tiempo.
Es imposible que
Es bueno que

• If the impersonal expression is one of truth or affirmation, use the indicative:

Es verdad que
Es cierto que } ella **llega** a tiempo.
No es dudoso que

10 Complete each of the following sentences with an appropriate word.

1. Es _____ que muchas personas no están al tanto de las noticias del mundo.

2. Además, es _____ que se lea el periódico.

3. Es _____ que la televisión puede ser muy educativa.

4. Es _____ que muchas personas encuentren aburridos los documentales.

5. Es _____ que a mucha gente le gusten los anuncios.

6. Es _____ la prensa nos diga la verdad.

11 Complete these sentences with the present indicative or the present subjunctive of the verbs in parentheses.

MARIO Mañana hay un documental muy interesante sobre la contaminación del aire.

TERESA Sí, ya lo sé. Es cierto que **(1)** _____ (ir) a ser muy interesante.

MARIO Es probable que mi familia y yo **(2)** _____ (ver) el programa.

TERESA Sí, es necesario que Uds. lo **(3)** _____ (ver). Es muy importante

que toda la gente **(4)** _____ (estar) al tanto de lo que está pasando.

MARIO Es evidente que muchas personas no **(5)** _____ (saber) ni jota de eso.

12 Write a sentence in reaction to each statement. Begin each sentence with an impersonal expression such as **es necesario que** or **es verdad que**.

1. Hay documentales sobre el béisbol.

_____

2. Los periódicos se hacen completamente electrónicos.

_____

3. Se puede sintonizar hasta 200 canales por cable.

_____

4. Las cadenas anuncian noticieros de tres horas.

_____

VOCABULARIO   El periódico   *Pupil's Edition, p. 205*

13 For each set of words, choose the word that doesn't belong and write it in the space provided.

_____ 1.	los titulares	la locutora	el comentarista
_____ 2.	los anuncios clasificados	los titulares	la primera plana
_____ 3.	el locutor	el artículo	los editoriales
_____ 4.	la sección de sociedad	la sección de moda	el periodista
_____ 5.	la sección del ocio	los obituarios	las tiras cómicas

14 For each description, write the section of the newspaper that would most likely interest that person.

la sección de sociedad	los titulares	las tiras cómicas
los editoriales	la sección de cocina	la sección de moda

_____ 1. Ricardo pasa mucho tiempo preparando comida. Siempre quiere experimentar con platos exquisitos.

_____ 2. A Esteban le importa cómo se ve. Se viste bien.

_____ 3. Clara es una mujer muy sofisticada e inteligente. Siempre asiste a todas las funciones publicitarias.

_____ 4. A Martín le gusta saber las opiniones de otras personas. Además, está loco por la política.

_____ 5. Los personajes favoritos de Matilde son Calvin y Hobbes.

_____ 6. Le gustan las noticias y los eventos importantes del mundo.

CAPÍTULO 9 Las apariencias engañan

■ PRIMER PASO

To express emotional reactions, you'll need to know specific vocabulary. To express disagreement, you'll need to use the subjunctive mood after disagreement and denial.

VOCABULARIO   Emotional reactions   *Pupil's Edition, p. 225*

1 Read each conversation and then use an expression to complete each statement.

reírse	quejarse	sentirse	alegrarse	enojarse

1.   ALEJANDRO   Cuéntame, María Elena. ¿Qué pasó entre tú y Pablo?

   MARÍA ELENA   Me dejó plantada en el cine ayer. No lo perdonaré.

   Ayer María Elena _____ con Pablo.

2.   SILVIA   ¿Qué pasó en tu clase de química ayer?

        MARTÍN   Es que el profesor Solé nos dio un día libre.

   Los estudiantes del profesor Solé _____ en la clase de química.

3.   GERARDO   ¿Por qué están enojados tus padres, Rosana?

        ROSANA   Por fin yo les dije que no es justo que yo sola haga todos los quehaceres.

   Rosana _____ de tener que hacer todos los quehaceres.

4.   ROBERTO   ¿Qué tal estuvo la fiesta de Teresa, Nena?

           NENA   Muy buena. Mario contó muchos chistes.

   Todos los invitados de Teresa _____ en la fiesta anoche.

2 Unscramble the following words.

PISTA	PALABRA REVUELTA
1. estar contento	**eaesglrar**
2. enfadarse	**renjaseo**
3. reaccionar a un chiste	**seeírr**
4. reírse de alguien	**ularserb**
5. enojarse	**aenadrsef**
6. estar	**rseentis**
7. nervioso	**ppreoocdua**

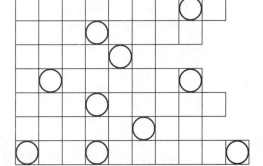

Now use the circled letters to find out how María Elena reacted when she dropped her baton during the school marching band's halftime show. (3 words)

_____

Gramática   The subjunctive after conjunctions   *Pupil's Edition, p. 226*
of time

1. When talking about future events or future plans, use the subjunctive mood after the following conjunctions: **cuando**, **después de que**, **en cuanto**, **hasta que**, **tan pronto como**, **en cuanto**.

    Mis amigos y yo pensamos ir al café **cuando termine** esta clase.

2. When talking about habitual events or completed past events, use the indicative after the same conjunctions.

    Cuando llegas, yo me voy.

    Cuando llegaste, yo me fui.

3. Always use the subjunctive mood after the following conjunctions: **a menos (de) que**, **antes (de) que**, **con tal (de) que**, **en caso de que**, and **para que**.

    En caso de que haya un examen mañana, vamos a estudiar.

3 Complete the following sentences with the more appropriate phrase of the two in parentheses.

1. Mañana _____ (hasta que / después de que) regresemos de la escuela, pienso salir a comer con mi familia.

2. Voy a traer el paraguas (*umbrella*) _____ (hasta que / en caso de que) llueva.

3. Siempre llueve _____ (hasta que / cuando) se me olvida el paraguas.

4. Nos sentimos muy nerviosos _____ (para que / en cuanto) el profesor nos dijo que había un examen.

5. Mis compañeros de clase y yo siempre nos quejamos _____ (hasta que / cuando) la profesora nos permite salir durante el recreo.

4 Complete the following conversation with an appropriate conjunction of time.

para que	en cuanto	cuando	antes de que	en caso de que

ANDRÉS   Diana, ¿cuándo nos va a poner el examen el profesor Williams?

DIANA   Dice que (1) _____ terminemos el capítulo cinco.

ANDRÉS   ¿Quieres estudiar esta noche (2) _____ nos lo ponga mañana?

DIANA   (3) _____ estudiemos, primero quiero terminar de leer el capítulo.

ANDRÉS   Bueno, llámame inmediatamente, (4) _____ termines

de leer el capítulo (5) _____ podamos comenzar.

CAPÍTULO 9 Primer paso

5 Complete the following paragraph with either the present indicative or the present subjunctive of the verb in parentheses.

Yo me enojo cuando la gente (1) _____ (burlarse) de mis amigos. Siempre cuando (2) _____ (llegar) Maribel a clase, los otros estudiantes se ríen de ella. Es que ella se viste diferente. En cuanto (3) _____ (comenzar) a burlarse, ella se pone roja. No sé qué aconsejarle. Tal vez ella pueda aprender a vestirse mejor, con tal de que ella no se (4) _____ (sentir) ofendida. De todas maneras va a ser así hasta que los otros estudiantes (5) _____ (aprender) a respetar a la gente diferente.

*G*ramática   The subjunctive with disagreement   *Pupil's Edition, p. 227*
and denial

Use the subjunctive mood after expressions of disagreement and denial such as
negar que and **no es verdad que**.

No es verdad que este libro **sea** aburrido.
Niego que los periodistas lo **sepan** todo.

6 Ramón disagrees with everything Al says. How would he respond to each of the following statements?

Al   Todos los estudiantes se burlan de mí.

RAMÓN   No es cierto que **(1)** _____ de ti.

Al   Todas las personas que hablan español son españolas.

RAMÓN   No es verdad que todos los hispanohablantes

(2) _____ españoles.

Al   Los jugadores de fútbol sacan las mejores notas de la clase.

RAMÓN   No estoy de acuerdo que ellos **(3)** _____ las mejores notas.

Al   Los músicos no trabajan tan fuerte como los atletas.

RAMÓN   No es verdad que los músicos no **(4)** _____ .

Al   Siempre hace calor en Texas.

RAMÓN   No es cierto que siempre **(5)** _____ calor allí.

7 Complete each of the following sentences with an appropriate expression from the box.

no es cierto	no es verdad	no niego	parece mentira	es cierto

1. _____ que los callados no sean inteligentes.

2. _____ que los atletas no puedan ser artísticos.

3. _____ que todos debemos comprender a los demás.

4. _____ que los norteamericanos siempre se quejen mucho.

5. _____ que hay discriminación en nuestro país.

8 Complete the paragraph with the correct indicative or subjunctive form of the verb in parentheses.

En nuestra escuela **(1)** _____ (haber) muchas controversias sobre las

distintas religiones que se representan. No niego que la gente **(2)** _____

(tener) sus propias ideas, pero no es cierto que nosotros no **(3)** _____

(apoyar) las culturas y religiones diferentes. Por ejemplo, nosotros

(4) _____ (tener) varios grupos étnicos aquí y cada uno

(5) _____ (tener) uno o dos representantes en el Consejo Estudiantil.

Nosotros negamos que esos representantes no **(6)** _____ (poder)

presentar sus opiniones cuando **(7)** _____ (querer).

9 Write out Fernando's thoughts from the following notes he has taken. Use the indicative or subjunctive as necessary.

1. mis padres / decir / los adolescentes / ser / flojo

_____

_____

2. yo / no creer / los jóvenes / no trabajar

_____

_____

3. no negar / algunos jóvenes / relajarse mucho

_____

_____

4. no ser verdad / mis amigos y yo / no trabajar

_____

_____

CAPÍTULO 9 Primer paso

VOCABULARIO   Descripciones de personalidades   *Pupil's Edition, p. 228*

10 Choose the word from the box that best completes each set and write it in the space provided.

> descortés   reírse   egoísta   tímido
> bobo   alegrarse

1. amigo: amigable:: malvado: _____

2. descortés: enojarse:: amigable: _____

3. callado: tímido:: torpe: _____

4. amigable: descortés:: generoso: _____

5. serio: alegrarse:: descortés: _____

6. presumido: arrogante:: callado: _____

11 Choose the word that best describes each of the following people and write it in the blank provided. Make each adjective agree.

> chismoso   callado   torpe   travieso
> descortés   egoísta   presumido

_____ 1. Sandra no habla mucho. Se aplica en todas sus clases pero nunca participa en las discusiones.

_____ 2. No hay quien aguante a Marilú. Ella cree que es la estudiante más inteligente del colegio.

_____ 3. Franco es buena gente pero no es la persona más inteligente ni ágil.

_____ 4. Nunca se les puede decir un secreto a Fernanda y Pablo. Se lo cuentan a todo el mundo.

_____ 5. Alicia trata muy mal a todos sus amigos. No se lleva bien con nadie.

_____ 6. Teresa no es nada generosa. Nunca comparte nada con sus amigos.

_____ 7. Iván y Lucía piensan que lo saben todo y siempre tratan de impresionar a la gente.

_____ 8. ¡Qué cómica es Alicia! Siempre nos reímos tanto con sus chistes e ideas locas.

■ SEGUNDO PASO

To express an assumption, you'll need to use some specific expressions. To make hypothetical statements, you'll need to use the conditional.

*G*ramática   The conditional   *Pupil's Edition, p. 233*

1. Verbs in the conditional express what would or might happen if something else were true:

Si tuviera tiempo, **iría** a la fiesta.   *If I had time, I would go.*

2. The conditional can also be used to make polite requests
¿Nos **podría** traer la cuenta?

3. The conditional is formed by adding the conditional endings to the stem of the verb. The stem for most verbs is the same as the infinitive.

COMPRAR	COMER	SERVIR
comprar**ía**	comer**ía**	servir**ía**
comprar**ías**	comer**ías**	servir**ías**
comprar**ía**	comer**ía**	servir**ía**
comprar**íamos**	comer**íamos**	servir**íamos**
comprar**íais**	comer**íais**	servir**íais**
comprar**ían**	comer**ían**	servir**ían**

4. The verbs that have irregular stems in the future tense have the same irregular stems in the conditional.

caber	**cabr-**	saber	**sabr-**	valer	**valdr-**
haber	**habr-**	poner	**pondr-**	venir	**vendr-**
poder	**podr-**	salir	**saldr-**	decir	**dir-**
querer	**querr-**	tener	**tendr-**	hacer	**har-**

12 Fill in the blanks in the following statements with the correct conditional form of the verb in parentheses.

1. Si tuviera más tiempo yo _____ (ir) al teatro con más frecuencia.

2. Si pudieras hablar italiano, _____ (poder) entender mejor las óperas.

3. Mis padres me dijeron que _____ (venir) conmigo para ver "Rigoletto".

4. No sé mucho de la ópera. Yo _____ (saber) más, pero sólo he ido a una.

5. A mis amigos les _____ (gustar) ir al teatro, pero cuesta mucho dinero.

6. Si pudiéramos, todos _____ (asistir) a más conciertos de la orquesta.

13 Complete the following paragraph with either the present indicative, the present subjunctive, or the conditional of the verb in parentheses, as required by the context.

Si yo pudiera vivir en la ciudad de Nueva York, lo **(1)** _____ (hacer).

Yo **(2)** _____ (vivir) en Staten Island. Me imagino que es muy tranquilo.

No **(3)** _____ (ir) a Brooklyn porque tengo la impresión de que

tiene mucha gente. No niego que Brooklyn **(4)** _____ (tener) secciones

bonitas pero no me gusta que **(5)** _____ (haber) mucha gente. Tengo un

amigo que vive en Manhattan. Él dice que le **(6)** _____ (gustar) irse de

Nueva York. Dice que **(7)** _____ (tener) mucha contaminación para él.

14 Complete the following survey by writing questions using the cues.

MODELO   Si Ud. pudiera vivir en cualquier país, . . . (dónde / vivir)
         ¿dónde viviría?

1. Si tú tuvieras más tiempo, . . . (dónde / pasarlo)

   _____

2. Si Ud. pudiera hacer un viaje a cualquier país, . . . (adónde / viajar)

   _____

3. Si Uds. tuvieran más dinero, . . . (qué / comprar)

   _____

4. Si Ud. pudiera estudiar un idioma extranjero, . . . (qué / estudiar)

   _____

5. Si tú pudieras cambiar el mundo, . . . (cómo / cambiarlo)

   _____

15 Your friend Mateo usually gives very direct commands. Rewrite each of the following commands using the conditional to soften them.

MODELO   Limpien Uds. la sala.   **¿Podrían limpiar la sala?**

1. Haz la cama.

   _____

2. Preparen Uds. el desayuno.

   _____

3. Niños, dense prisa en el baño.

   _____

4. Salgamos temprano para la escuela.

   _____

VOCABULARIO La discriminación *Pupil's Edition, p. 234*

16 Unscramble the following words.

PISTA	PALABRA REVUELTA
1. la condición de no saber	cignranoia
2. necesidad	alfat
3. no a favor	ne tcnrao
4. disposición	datituc
5. no la mayoría	íioranm
6. flojo	oreezosp
7. opinión ignorante	ureiciojp

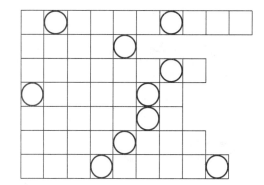

Now unscramble the circled letters to find out what Andreas wouldn't do if he met someone who had different customs. (2 words)

_____

17 Complete the following paragraph with an appropriate word or expression from the box. Conjugate any verbs as necessary.

> combatir   juzgar   darse cuenta
> minoría   estereotipos
> ignorancia   discriminación   prejuicio   respetar

Un problema grave en los Estados Unidos es el que existe entre los distintos

grupos étnicos, o sea, el **(1)** _____ . Es que muchos no saben o

todavía no **(2)** _____ de que la minoría ha tenido que combatir

mucha **(3)** _____ . Por ejemplo, la mayoría tiende a creer en

(4) _____ , ideas exageradas de cómo son las personas de cierto
grupo étnico. Un ejemplo sería la idea de que todos los hispanos tienen familias grandes.

De todas maneras, hay que **(5)** _____ esta ignorancia. Todos

tenemos que **(6)** _____ las costumbres de otras personas y de

otras culturas. Tampoco debemos **(7)** _____ a nadie antes de que

lo conozcamos. Esto se llama el **(8)** _____ , y no es justo.

CAPÍTULO 9 Segundo paso

10 La riqueza cultural

■ PRIMER PASO

To talk about accomplishments, you'll need to use related vocabulary and expressions.
To talk about future plans, you'll need to use the subjunctive after certain conjunctions.

VOCABULARIO   El éxito   *Pupil's Edition, p. 250*

1 Match each word in the box to its definition. Write each word in the blank provided.

> el esfuerzo   alcanzar   la aportación   agradecido   el reto   el éxito   orgulloso

_____ 1. el obstáculo que uno tiene que superar para tener éxito

_____ 2. lo que consigues después de aplicarte a un proyecto

_____ 3. cómo se siente uno al tener éxito o al superarse

_____ 4. cómo se siente uno al decir "gracias"

_____ 5. la aplicación o la dedicación que resulta en el éxito

_____ 6. conseguir después de mucho esfuerzo

2 Complete the following paragraph with an appropriate word from the box. Conjugate any verbs as necessary.

> agradecido   esfuerzo   alcanzar   éxito   retos   orgulloso   superarse

Me siento muy (1) _____ de las aportaciones de mi familia. Mis padres, que son de Michigan, vinieron a España hace 10 años. Cuando llegaron, había muchos (2) _____ que ellos tenían que superar. Después de dos años ellos (3) _____ a dominar el español. Además, me han hablado en inglés para que yo lo pueda hablar también. Estoy muy (4) _____ por eso. Hablando dos idiomas, voy a tener más (5) _____.

3 Write a logical completion for each of the following sentences using an appropriate phrase from the box. Conjugate verbs as needed and add any necessary words.

MODELO   Cuando saqué una "A" en el examen de química mis padres...
se sintieron muy orgullosos de mí.

> aportar a la cultura estadounidense   estar agradecido
>
> superarse   poner todo mi esfuerzo en estudiarlo   tener éxito

1. Es necesario trabajar mucho para...

   _____

2. Pienso tener éxito en la universidad. De esta manera yo...

   _____

3. Cuando mis padres me regalaron un reloj para mi graduación, yo...

   _____

4. Para dominar el francés...

   _____

5. Mi familia y yo estamos muy orgullosos de todo lo que...

   _____

VOCABULARIO   Las raíces   *Pupil's Edition, p. 251*

4 Use the clues in the first column to unscramble the words in the second column.

PISTA	PALABRA REVUELTA
1. carácter personal	odmo ed rse
2. hábito cultural	muertoscb
3. los orígenes étnicos	asl sícrae
4. obligación	pcismmrooo
5. preservar	rtemanne
6. llevarse bien	aenrcja
7. crecer	cirsear

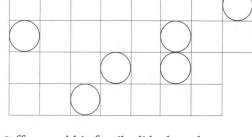

Now use the circled letters to find out what Jeffrey and his family did when they moved to Colombia. (2 words)

_____

5 Complete the conversation between Alicia and Manolo with an appropriate word from the box. Conjugate any verbs as necessary.

asimilarse		raíces	mantener
	encajar		
compromiso		modo de ser	costumbres

ALICIA   Manolo, ¿de dónde eres?

MANOLO   Bueno, soy estadounidense, pero tengo (1) _____ peruanas. Es que mi papá se crió en Perú.

ALICIA   ¿De veras? ¿Observan Uds. (2) _____ peruanas en casa?

MANOLO   De vez en cuando. Pero hacemos mucho al estilo americano. Mis padres

(3) _____ cuando llegaron a los Estados Unidos.

ALICIA   Sí, pero es importante no perder la cultura hispana. Hay que

(4) _____la, ¿no?

MANOLO   Claro. No hemos olvidado nuestra cultura, pero también queremos

(5) _____ con nuestros amigos norteamericanos.

*G*ramática de repaso   The subjunctive with certain conjunctions   *Pupil's Edition, p. 253*

1. When talking about future events or future plans, use the subjunctive mood after the following conjunctions: **cuando**, **después de que**, **hasta que**, **tan pronto como**, and **en cuanto**.

   Quiero viajar a Bolivia **tan pronto como termine** mis estudios.

2. Always use the subjunctive mood after the following conjunctions: **a menos (de) que**, **antes de que**, **con tal (de) que**, **en caso de que**, and **para que**.

   Antes de que viajes a Bolivia, quiero que nos reunamos.

6 Ana María is very busy with her friends. As she tells you what they do together, indicate whether the sentences are talking about **a)** future events, **b)** habitual events, or **c)** completed past events.

_____ 1. Ana María y yo comemos juntas cuando podemos.

_____ 2. Por ejemplo, mañana vamos a encontrarnos en la cafetería cuando terminen nuestras clases.

_____ 3. Ayer pudimos reunirnos en cuanto asistimos a la asamblea.

_____ 4. En cuanto llegue Ana María, vamos a la cafetería.

_____ 5. Muchas veces nos quedamos allí conversando hasta que tenemos que regresar a clase.

_____ 6. Pero hoy, después de que almorcemos, quiero ir al parque a dar un paseo.

7 Conjugate the verb in parentheses in the present indicative if the sentence is talking about habitual events, or in the present subjunctive if it's talking about future events.

1. Siempre estudio en la biblioteca después de que _____ (terminar) las clases.

2. Cuando _____ (cumplir) los 16 años espero sacar la licencia de manejar.

3. Tan pronto como _____ (ser) mayor, estudiaré para ser médico.

4. Me gusta ayudar a la gente cuando _____ (poder).

5. Jorge quiere jugar al fútbol hasta que _____ (graduarse).

6. Ofelia siempre estudia tan pronto como _____ (regresar) de la escuela.

8 Write the more appropriate expression of the two in parentheses.

CELIA ¿Qué quieres ser **(1)** _____ (cuando / con tal de que) seas mayor?

GABI No sé. Quería ser médica **(2)** _____ (cuando / antes de que) era niña, pero en cuanto me di cuenta de lo difícil que era... Y tú, ¿qué quieres ser?

CELIA Yo no sé tampoco. No voy a tomar la decisión **(3)** _____ (con tal de que / hasta que) vaya a la universidad.

GABI Sí, pero **(4)** _____ (con tal de que / antes de que) comiences a asistir, tienes que tener una idea.

CELIA Bueno, **(5)** _____ (en caso de que / antes de que) sea necesario, les voy a decir que quiero estudiar la arquitectura.

GABI Buena idea, pero sólo **(6)** _____ (para que / con tal de que) te guste.

9 Complete each sentence by adding a conjunction of time and forming a logical phrase with the cues in parentheses. Use each conjunction only once.

MODELO Martín y sus amigos quieren hacer una fiesta... (él / irse a la universidad)
...antes de que él se vaya a la universidad.

después de que	tan pronto como	hasta que	con tal de que	cuando

1. Martín piensa hacer muchos nuevos amigos... (él / asistir a la universidad)

_____

2. Martín y sus padres quieren ver la residencia estudiantil... (ellos / visitar la universidad)

_____

3. Martín no va a comprar sus textos... (él / comenzar sus clases)

_____

4. Los estudiantes universitarios van a buscar trabajos profesionales... (ellos / graduarse)

_____

5. Todos pueden asistir a la universidad... (ellos / terminar sus estudios secundarios)

_____

■ SEGUNDO PASO

To express cause and effect, you'll need to use infinitives after prepositions, and you'll need to know some specific vocabulary. To express intention and purpose, you'll need to use **para** followed by an infinitive and **para que** followed by the subjunctive.

> ## Nota *G*ramatical Infinitives after prepositions *Pupil's Edition, p. 257*
> When a verb comes immediately after any preposition (**por**, **para**, **con**, **en**, **a**, **de**, etc.), it is always left in the infinitive form. In phrases like these, the infinitive is often equivalent to the *-ing* form of the verb in English:
> Llámame **antes de venir**. *before coming*
> César sueña **con ser** pintor. *dreams of being*

10 Magdalena is giving a speech at a local conference. Complete her speech with the correct preposition from the box. Some prepositions may be used more than once.

> por   en   de   a   con   para

Gracias a todos (1) _____ venir a esta conferencia. Hoy vamos

(2) _____ hablar de varios problemas que afectan a los hispanos de nuestra

comunidad. Primero, somos muchos que todavía no hemos aprendido (3) _____

hablar inglés. Tengo la impresión de que no lo aprendemos (4) _____ vivir en

comunidades de habla española. Pero ya no se puede contar (5) _____

mantenernos separados. Yo vengo aquí con la idea (6) _____ convencernos de

ir a clases. Todos debemos tratar (7) _____ asistir a una clase cada semana.

11 Complete each of the following sentences with either the present subjunctive, the present indicative, or the infinitive form of the verb in parentheses.

1. Toda mi vida he soñado con _____ (ser) doctora.

2. Todos mis amigos y yo vamos a _____ (asistir) a la universidad.

3. Ya hablo español e inglés; por lo tanto yo _____ (querer) estudiar chino.

4. Antes de _____ (comenzar) a _____ (asistir) a clases, quiero viajar.

5. Quiero viajar a Australia para _____ (practicar) el inglés.

6. Después de que yo _____ (regresar) de Australia, mis abuelos van a visitarnos.

7. Mis padres van a regalarme dinero para mi cumpleaños para que yo

   _____ (poder) pagar la matrícula.

12 Sergio is making signs for his school. How would he tell someone...?

1. that reading is fun

   _____

2. that running in the halls isn't permitted (**no se permite**)

   _____

3. to wash hands before eating

   _____

4. thank you for not talking in the library

   _____

VOCABULARIO Cómo realizar las metas *Pupil's Edition, p. 258*

13 Rodolfo went to see the guidance counselor at his school. Complete each sentence with an appropriate expression from the box. Conjugate any verbs as necessary.

> a cabo aspirar esforzarse la meta
>
> realizar soñar tomar la iniciativa

1. Es necesario aplicarse para _____ un sueño.

2. Muchas personas no tienen éxito por no llevar _____ sus objetivos.

3. Ser médico es difícil pero puedo lograrlo si _____ por estudiar mucho.

4. Siempre quise ir a la universidad. ¿Con qué _____ tú?

5. Ayer nadie quería hablar de nuestro problema así que yo_____.

6. Mi papá ha tenido mucho éxito como artista. Y yo _____ a sus éxitos.

14 Mari and Beto are talking about their future. Complete their conversation by circling the more appropriate word in parentheses.

MARI ¿Qué (**1**) (aspiraciones / iniciativas) tienes para el futuro?

BETO No sé. Quiero (**2**) (enfocarme / soñar) en mis estudios secundarios antes de pensar en el futuro. Y tú, ¿qué objetivos quieres (**3**) (tomar la iniciativa / llevar a cabo)?

MARI Yo también quiero terminar mis estudios, pero ya es hora de (**4**) (lograr / tomar la iniciativa) si quiero asistir a la universidad.

BETO Tienes razón, pero ahora tengo malas notas. Primero tengo que (**5**) (esforzarme / realizar) por sacar mejores notas.

MARI Claro. Y si te aplicas, lo vas a (**6**) (soñar / lograr).

¿Te acuerdas? Reflexive pronouns *Pupil's Edition, p. 258*

When using a reflexive verb, the reflexive pronoun must always agree with the subject, stated or implied.

esforzarse → **Yo** (*stated subject*) **me** esforcé por sacar mejores notas.

enfocarse → Tienes (*implied subject* **tú**) que enfocar**te** en tus estudios.

15 Diana has written some notes for her composition about the importance of studying. Complete each sentence with the correct reflexive pronoun.

1. Mis padres dicen que es importante que yo _____ enfoque en mis estudios.

2. Mi amigo Arturo saca malas notas así que yo le recomiendo que _____ esfuerce por estudiar más.

3. Le digo "si quieres salir bien en la escuela, tienes que dejar de quejar_____."

4. Estudiar es una manera en que uno _____ supera.

5. Cuando mis padres vinieron a los Estados Unidos del Ecuador, _____ esforzaron por asimilar_____.

6. _____ crié en los Estados Unidos pero mis padres y yo _____ sentimos muy orgullosos de nuestras raíces ecuatorianas.

16 María Pepa is interviewing Sebastián for the school paper. Conjugate each verb as necessary.

MARÍA PEPA   Dime, Sebastián, ¿en qué país **(1)** _____ (criarse)?

SEBASTIÁN   Aquí en los Estados Unidos, pero **(2)** _____ (sentirse) muy orgulloso de mis raíces argentinas. Mis abuelos vinieron aquí para

(3) _____ (superarse).

MARÍA PEPA   ¿Cómo **(4)** _____ (sentirse) cuando llegaron?

¿Tuvieron que hacer un esfuerzo por

(5) _____ (asimilarse)?

SEBASTIÁN   No sé. Eso fue hace muchos años. Por lo menos les fue bastante difícil

(6) _____ (despedirse) de su país.

MARÍA PEPA   ¿Y qué planes tienes tú para el futuro, Sebastián? ¿A qué piensas

(7) _____ (dedicarse)?

SEBASTIÁN   No tengo la menor idea. Creo que es buena idea

(8) _____ (enfocarse) en mis estudios.

17 Your pen pal in Buenos Aires wants to know about the study habits that you and your friends follow. Can you express each of the following in Spanish?

1. My friends and I have made an effort to make better grades.

   _____

   _____

2. I don't like to complain about making bad grades.

   _____

   _____

3. Our objective is to focus on our studies.

   _____

   _____

4. After graduating, we hope to be able to go to college.

   _____

   _____

---

*G*ramática de repaso   Subjunctive with **para que**   *Pupil's Edition, p. 260*

The preposition **para** is often followed by the infinitive of a verb to express purpose or intent. Use **para** if there is no change of subject.

   Los estudiantes estudian **para aprender**.

The expression **para que** also expresses purpose or intent but is only necessary when there is a change of subject (**el profesor** and **los estudiantes**, for example). It is always followed by a verb in the subjunctive mood.

   El profesor enseña **para que** los estudiantes **aprendan**.

---

18 Fernando will be graduating this year and is writing about his future plans. Complete each sentence with either **para** or **para que** as required by the context.

Este año escolar es muy importante (1) _____ mí y mis amigos. Es mi último año antes de ir a la universidad. Pienso estudiar mucho (2) _____ sacar buenas notas. Mi familia ha hecho muchas cosas (3) _____ ayudar. Por ejemplo, mis padres me han dado una habitación privada (4) _____ yo pueda estudiar en silencio. Mi hermano ha ofrecido hacer algunos de mis quehaceres (5) _____ tenga más tiempo (6) _____ estudiar.

19 Mario is getting ready to take a trip to Spain. How would he...?

1. tell a friend he wants to go to Spain to meet people

_____

_____

2. say his school has given him a week so that he can go

_____

_____

3. say he and his friends are going together to have fun

_____

_____

4. say his parents have given them some information so they'll learn more about the country

_____

_____

20 As Alejandro tells you about his upcoming shopping trip, complete each sentence with a phrase with **para** + infinitive or **para que** + subjunctive to indicate purpose. Use the cues in parentheses.

1. Hoy todos vamos al centro comercial... (hacer compras)

_____

_____

2. Mi papá me ha dado 10 dólares... (yo / comprarle / una camiseta)

_____

_____

3. Mi amigo Mario va a usar el coche de su papá... (nosotros / no tener que ir en autobús)

_____

_____

4. Juanita quiere ir también... (mirar las vitrinas)

_____

5. Mi mamá no quiere que pase mucho tiempo allí... (yo / no gastar mucho dinero)

_____

_____

CAPÍTULO 11

El mundo en que vivimos

PRIMER PASO

To point out problems and their consequences, you'll need to use some specific vocabulary. You'll also need to use the impersonal **se**. To talk about how you would solve a problem, you'll need to use the conditional.

VOCABULARIO   Los problemas sociales   *Pupil's Edition, p. 279*

1 Use the clues in the first column to unscramble the words in the second column.

PISTA	PALABRA REVUELTA
1. falta de trabajo	**eemsepdlo**
2. falta de comida	**emabrh**
3. un hombre que roba	**ólarnd**
4. malestar	**dmnereadfe**
5. hacer (un crimen)	**reecomt**
6. asesinato	**oiohdimci**
7. campaña	**graoarpm**

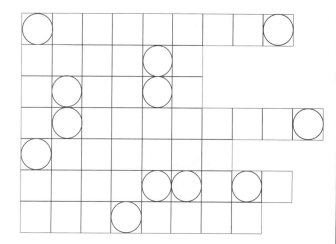

Now unscramble the circled letters to find out what the biggest social problem in Celestina's home town is. (1 word)

_____

2 Write each of the following problems under a logical category.

la delincuencia   el hambre   el aumento de precios   la enfermedad
la drogadicción   el desempleo   el homicidio

Crimen	Problema de salud	Problema económico

3 For each conversation, write the problem that is being talked about. Include the definite article.

_____ 1. MARI ¿Qué les pasó anoche, Gabi?

GABI Es que entró un ladrón. Se llevó nuestro televisor.

_____ 2. FELIPE Siento mucho que tu tío haya muerto, Mario; mi más sentido pésame.

MARIO Gracias, Felipe. Estuvo enfermo por mucho tiempo. Por lo menos ya no sufre.

_____ 3. CLAUDIA Según el gobierno, hoy en día hay más personas que no tienen qué comer.

BERTA Es imposible creer, ¿no?

_____ 4. PÁMELA Si no realizamos campañas preventivas contra las drogas, lo lamentaremos.

DIANA Tienes razón, Pamela. Es un problema muy serio.

_____ 5. SERGIO Se dice que el homicidio ha aumentado.

MATILDE Y lo peor es que las víctimas son muy jóvenes.

¿Te acuerdas? Impersonal **se** *Pupil's Edition, p. 279*

In a sentence that talks about what people in general do, **se** can replace the subjects **uno**, **la gente**, **ellos**, **nosotros**, **muchos** and any other subject that doesn't refer to a specific person. The verb usually becomes singular.

Antes, la gente caminaba más. → Antes, **se** caminaba más.

Dicen que el profesor Smith es difícil. → **Se** dice que el profesor Smith es difícil.

---

4 Rewrite the underlined phrases in each of the following sentences using the impersonal **se**.

1. La gente dice que la criminalidad ha aumentado.

_____

2. Ellos creen que la contaminación no es un problema serio.

_____

3. Antes nosotros no producíamos tanta contaminación ecológica.

_____

4. Durante los años 50, uno pasaba más tiempo con la familia.

_____

5. Hoy, muchos combaten la delincuencia.

_____

6. La gente ha actuado para reducir el homicidio.

_____

5 Elsbieta would like to vary the style in her speech for Environmental Awareness Week. Help her by underlining the six phrases that could be rewritten using the impersonal **se.** Then rewrite them in the spaces below.

> *Es evidente que la contaminación es un problema muy serio. Sin embargo, muchas personas pueden hacer mucho para mejorar la situación. Es fácil. Uno sólo tiene que hacer algunas cosas muy sencillas. En primer lugar, nosotros debemos manejar menos nuestros coches. También nosotros podemos reciclar el papel, el aluminio y las botellas de vidrio. Además, si la gente habla de lo fácil que es, muchos comenzarán a reciclar más.*

1. _____   4. _____

2. _____   5. _____

3. _____   6. _____

6 Rogelio is writing a questionnaire to find out what things used to be like. Using the verbs in parentheses, how would he ask...?

1. where people used to live (**vivir**)

   ¿ _____
   _____ ?

2. if people used to worry about the environment (**preocuparse**)

   ¿ _____
   _____ ?

3. when people noticed the pollution problem (**fijarse**)

   ¿ _____
   _____ ?

4. what everyone did to solve the problem (**hacer**)

   ¿ _____
   _____ ?

5. if one is more informed today about these problems (**estar mejor informado**)

   ¿ _____
   _____ ?

¿Se te ha olvidado? The conditional *Pupil's Edition, p. 281*

Verbs in the conditional express what one *would* do or what *would* happen if circumstances were different. To form it, add the conditional endings to the stem of the verb. The infinitive serves as the stem of most verbs in the conditional. Verbs with irregular stems are listed on page 347 of your textbook.

COMETER

yo cometer**ía** nosotros cometer**íamos**
tú cometer**ías** vosotros cometer**íais**
él / ella / Ud. cometer**ía** ellos / ellas / Uds. cometer**ían**

7 Complete each of the following sentences with the conditional of the verb in parentheses.

1. Si pudiera hacerlo, yo _____ (intentar) eliminar la pobreza.

2. Mis padres me _____ (dar) el dinero para asistir a la universidad si lo tuvieran.

3. Si no tuviéramos campañas contra las drogas, lo _____. (lamentar)

4. Hace diez años los científicos nos dijeron que nosotros _____ (tener) muchos problemas ecológicos.

5. Si todos pudieran reciclar, _____ (haber) menos basura en el mundo.

8 Complete the following conversation between Rosario and Raquel by conjugating the verb in parentheses in either the conditional or the imperfect as required by the context.

ROSARIO Oye, Raquel, ¿qué (1) _____ (hacer) tú si tuvieras más tiempo para divertirte?

RAQUEL No sé, de niña me (2) _____ (gustar) mucho ir a la playa.

Creo que (3) _____ (ir) más a la playa, si tuviera más tiempo.

ROSARIO ¿De veras? Cuando yo (4) _____ (ser) niña, mis amigos y yo (5) _____ (pasar) mucho tiempo jugando en el parque.

A mí me (6) _____ (gustar) jugar más con mis amigos hoy en día.

RAQUEL Me acuerdo que tú y yo (7) _____ (tener) muchos

problemas en la escuela porque jugábamos más y (8) _____ (estudiar) menos.

ROSARIO Es cierto. Nuestras notas de hoy no (9) _____ (ser) tan buenas si no nos aplicáramos tanto.

RAQUEL Y nosotras (10) _____ (tener) que dedicar aun más tiempo a nuestros estudios hoy por no haber aprendido lo de antes.

SEGUNDO PASO

To talk about hypothetical situations, you'll need to know some specific expressions. You'll also need to use the past subjunctive in contrary-to-fact phrases.

ASÍ SE DICE   Talking about hypothetical situations   *Pupil's Edition, p. 286*

9 Indicate whether each of the following sentences is talking about **a)** a hypothetical situation, or **b)** an actual situation.

_____ 1. Si hubiera paz en el mundo, menos personas morirían.

_____ 2. No hago mucho por el medio ambiente porque no tengo tiempo.

_____ 3. Si te aplicaras más, podrías sacar mejores notas.

_____ 4. Si yo fuera presidente, haría muchos cambios.

_____ 5. Nuestro gobierno no hace lo suficiente para proteger el medio ambiente.

_____ 6. ¡Qué bueno sería si encontráramos una solución para la contaminación!

_____ 7. La gente maneja sus coches demasiado. Por eso el aire está contaminado.

10 For each of the following statements about actual situations, write the beginning of a sentence expressing what might happen if . . . Use an expression for hypothetical situations.

MODELO   No hay paz en el mundo. (haber paz . . .)

         Pero si hubiera paz . . .

1. Hay muchas enfermedades en el mundo. (encontrarse una cura . . .)

_____

2. Es imposible cambiar el mundo. (yo / poder / cambiarlo . . .)

_____

3. Nuestra ciudad es muy pequeña y no tiene transporte público. (nosotros / vivir / en una ciudad más grande . . .)

_____

4. Hay muchas compañías que no hacen nada que proteja el medio ambiente. (yo / tener mi propia compañía . . .)

_____

5. Nuestro presidente no hace mucho para bajar la drogadicción. (yo / ser presidente o presidenta . . .)

_____

6. Muchas personas no usan transporte público. (ellos / vivir en una ciudad grande . . .)

_____

¿Se te ha olvidado? The preterite *Pupil's Edition, p. 336–356*

1. You've used the preterite tense to talk about things
   - that happened in the past from start to finish:
     Ayer lo **pasamos** bien en la playa.
   - that happened for specific periods of time:
     Mis amigos **estuvieron** en mi casa **por dos horas**.
2. It's also possible to use the preterite with **nunca** to indicate that something was never true, or never happened even once:
   Nunca fui a España.

11 Orieta is giving a presentation to her neighborhood committee on the environment. Complete her speech with the correct preterite form of the verb in parentheses.

El año pasado, nuestra comunidad **(1)** _____ (hacer) mucho para

comenzar a proteger el medio ambiente. Por ejemplo, nosotros **(2)** _____ (realizar) una campaña para bajar la contaminación. Ahora la gente que nunca

(3) _____ (usar) transporte público lo usa todas las semanas. Los

políticos **(4)** _____ (dedicarse) a construir centros de reciclaje de papel y

de vidrio. Además, nosotros **(5)** _____ (poner) recipientes de basura en

todas las calles. Y por fin, los científicos **(6)** _____ (esforzarse) por encontrar maneras de bajar la contaminación causada por las fábricas.

12 Complete this conversation between Manuel and Víctor with the correct preterite form of the verb in parentheses.

MANUEL ¿Sabías que unos ladrones **(1)** _____ (entrar) en la casa de los
Pérez ayer mientras ellos estaban en el cine?

VÍCTOR ¡Ay, no me digas! ¿Qué **(2)** _____ (pasar)?

MANUEL Los ladrones les **(3)** _____ (robar) el televisor y unas joyas. Los

Pérez **(4)** _____ (estar) muy enojados.

VÍCTOR ¡Qué lástima! ¿Ellos **(5)** _____ (llamar) a la policía?

MANUEL Sí. Los policías les **(6)** _____ (decir) que

(7) _____ (ser) los mismos ladrones que **(8)** _____
(cometer) otros robos en el barrio.

VÍCTOR Yo creía que sus vecinos ya **(9)** _____ (realizar) una campaña hace
un mes para combatir el robo.

MANUEL Iban a hacerlo, ¡pero nunca lo **(10)** _____ (hacer)!

13 Complete these sentences saying what caused each situation. Use the preterite tense.

1. Hay mucha contaminación en el aire porque. . . . (gente / manejar / demasiado / coches)

_____

2. Muchas personas tienen hambre porque. . . . (gobierno / no realizar / campaña / para / pobres)

_____

3. Hay más casos de enfermedades serias debido a que. . . . (médicos / no promover / educación de salud)

_____

4. El homicidio está bajando puesto que. . . . (policías / implementar / programa de seguridad)

_____

---

*G*ramática   Past subjunctive in contrary-to-fact   *Pupil's Edition, p. 287*
clauses

1. To form the past subjunctive, drop the **-on** of the third person plural preterite form of the verb and add the following endings. **estar → estuvieron → estuvier-**

que yo estuvier**a**	que nosotros estuviér**amos**
que tú estuvier**as**	que vosotros estuvierais
que él / ella / Ud. estuvier**a**	que ellos / ellas / Uds. estuvier**an**

2. The past subjunctive after **si** (*if*) expresses a wish that things were the opposite of the way they really are. It's often followed by the conditional.

Si **fuera** posible (*pero no es posible*), enseñaría a la gente a no juzgar.

---

14 The following sentences talk about what will happen if certain things come true. Rewrite them so that they talk about what would happen.

MODELO   Si tenemos el tiempo, estudiaremos. **Si tuviéramos el tiempo, estudiaríamos.**

1. Si está lloviendo, no iremos al parque.

_____

2. Si te aplicas, te superarás.

_____

3. Si estudiamos juntas, sacaremos mejores notas.

_____

4. Si es posible, saldremos a comer esta noche.

_____

5. Si puedo salir, te llamaré.

_____

15 Marvin is doing a survey to find out what would need to be true for the following things to happen. He's asked several volunteers to complete the following sentences. How would you complete each sentence? Use the past subjunctive of an appropriate expression from the box.

aplicarse	hacer la tarea	dar un paseo por el parque
conocer a más gente	trabajar	estudiar tener el dinero

1. Yo compraría un coche nuevo si . . .

_____

2. Mi hermana sacaría mejores notas si . . .

_____

3. Tendrías más dinero si . . .

_____

4. Sería muy romántico si mi novio(a) y yo . . .

_____

5. Los estudiantes podrían contestar las preguntas si . . .

_____

16 Calvin is daydreaming about how nice things would be if only certain things were true. Write what he wishes by using **si** and the past subjunctive of the underlined verb.

MODELO   No <u>hay</u> tiempo para ver televisión.

¡Pero si hubiera tiempo. . . !

1. No <u>llueve</u> chocolate.

_____

2. <u>Tengo</u> que ir a la escuela todos los días.

_____

3. Mi clase de latín <u>es</u> muy difícil.

_____

4. No <u>hay</u> tiempo para ver televisión.

_____

5. <u>Es</u> imposible sacar buenas notas sin estudiar.

_____

6. Mi novia no me <u>da</u> regalos.

_____

CAPÍTULO 12 Mis planes para el futuro

■ PRIMER PASO

To talk about former jobs and goals, you'll need to know vocabulary for careers and professions. You'll also need to use the preterite and imperfect tenses together. To talk about future career plans, you'll need to use **ir a** + infinitive and the future tense.

VOCABULARIO   Las carreras y los oficios   *Pupil's Edition, p.303*

1 Simón is trying to recommend future careers for some students at his high school. For each of the following descriptions, write the profession that would best suit that person.

> trabajador(a) social   abogado(a)   carpintero(a)
>
> escritor(a)   periodista   técnico(a) de computadoras

_____ 1. A Hortensia le gusta mucho discutir. Defiende a todos sus amigos cuando la gente les acusa de algo.

_____ 2. Sandra se mantiene al tanto de todo. Es un poco chismosa.

_____ 3. Sara piensa de una manera muy lógica. También le gusta trabajar con equipo electrónico.

_____ 4. David es muy creativo. Tiene una imaginación muy impresionante. Le gusta leer novelas también.

_____ 5. A Esperanza le encanta diseñar cosas con las manos. El año pasado construyó una casa en miniatura muy bonita.

_____ 6. Mario es muy buen consejero. Siempre sabe qué aconsejarles a sus amigos cuando tienen problemas.

2 With whom might each professional in the first column work?

_____ 1. abogado   **a.** doctora

_____ 2. arquitecta   **b.** carpintero

_____ 3. contador   **c.** policía

_____ 4. técnico de computadoras   **d.** científica

_____ 5. farmacéutico   **e.** comerciante

_____ 6. vendedora   **f.** banquero

_____ 7. escritor   **g.** trabajador social

_____ 8. sicólogo   **h.** periodista

Gramática de repaso   Preterite and imperfect   *Pupil's Edition, p. 304*

- Verbs in the preterite talk about individual events or states in the past that each happened from start to finish or for specific periods of time.

    Ayer **hicimos** una fiesta y **celebramos** todo el día.

- Verbs in the imperfect talk about habitual events in the past that took place on a regular basis and also describe characteristics or conditions in the past. Always use the imperfect of **ser** to tell time in the past and the imperfect of **tener** to tell a person's age in the past.

    Cada año mis compañeros de clase me **hacían** una fiesta.

    Yo **estaba** muy contenta.

    María Elena **era** muy gorda cuando **tenía** 10 años.

- Used together, the imperfect describes background settings (time of day, weather, where people and things were, what they were doing, etc.) and the preterite expresses what happened in that setting.

    Dábamos un paseo por el parque cuando **vimos** el OVNI.

3 Complete each sentence with the preterite or the imperfect of the verb in parentheses.

1. Ayer mi familia y yo _____ (decidir) hacer un viaje a Colima.

2. Hicimos el viaje porque _____ (querer) visitar a mis tíos.

3. Mis tíos se alegraron cuando ellos _____ (saber) que veníamos.

4. Cuando nos fuimos _____ (hacer) muy buen tiempo.

5. _____ (Ser) las nueve de la mañana cuando nos fuimos.

6. El viaje _____ (ser) muy largo. Duró tres horas.

7. Mientras papá _____ (manejar), nosotros _____ (leer).

8. Al principio mi hermano no _____ (querer) venir, pero luego decidió que sí.

4 Mark is writing an essay for his Spanish class about what he wanted to be when he was young. Complete his paragraph with either the preterite or imperfect of the verb in parentheses.

Cuando (1) _____ (tener) diez años, (2) _____ (querer) ser científico al ser grande. Todos mis familiares siempre me (3) _____ (decir) que sería muy difícil. Pero yo (4) _____ (estar) empeñado. Entonces, cuando (5) _____ (tener) 13 años, (6) _____ (comenzar) la escuela secundaria. Allí (7) _____ (tomar) muchos cursos de ciencias para prepararme para la universidad. Cuando por fin (8) _____ (asistir) a la universidad, ya (9) _____ (estar) bien preparado para el programa de científicos.

5 Read the following story that Patricia wrote for her Spanish class. Indicate whether the underlined verbs are describing the background information or if they relate a specific event of the story. Write each verb in the appropriate column.

> Cuando vivía con mis tíos en Managua, íbamos con ellos al centro de la ciudad. Me acuerdo de una vez especial. Fuimos al centro y nos reunimos en un café. Ese día hacía mucho sol así que decidimos tomar el café afuera. Mientras hablábamos pasó un hombre por nuestra mesa. Era un hombre muy alto y guapo. Llevaba una bolsa negra. Nosotros le dimos un vistazo y de repente sacó una cámara de su bolsa y sacó una foto de nosotros. Entonces el hombre corrió del café. Al día siguiente vimos nuestra foto en el periódico "El Barricada". Debajo de la foto decía "La familia real española visita Nicaragua".

Background information

1. _____
2. _____
3. _____
4. _____

Specific event

1. _____
2. _____
3. _____
4. _____
5. _____

6 Fill in each of the following blanks with either the preterite or the imperfect of **querer, saber,** or **conocer.**

> Por fin, mi novia Alicia (**1**) _____ a mis padres.
>
> Yo (**2**) _____ que ella les caería bien. Ella no
>
> (**3**) _____ conocerlos porque estaba nerviosa pero
>
> cuando ellos (**4**) _____ que ella venía a mi fiesta,
>
> insistieron en conocerla. Cuando yo (**5**) _____ a Alicia
>
> por primera vez (**6**) _____ presentársela a mis padres
>
> pero no pude. Después de eso, mis padres siempre se quejaban porque yo
>
> hablaba mucho de ella y aunque ellos (**7**) _____ quién
>
> era, no la (**8**) _____ .

¡Ven conmigo! Level 3, Chapter 12 Grammar and Vocabulary Workbook **97**
HRW material copyrighted under notice appearing earlier in this work.
CAPÍTULO 12 Primer paso

7 You witnessed a robbery while you were shopping at the mall today. The police are counting on you to tell them what happened. Write sentences recounting the whole event. Use the preterite and imperfect as necessary.

1. ser / las tres y media

   _____

2. mis amigos y yo / caminar / por el centro comercial

   _____

3. yo / hacer / compras / con mis amigos

   _____

4. nosotros / estar / cansado

   _____

5. de repente / nosotros / ver / a dos hombres

   _____

6. ellos / tener / dos cajas

   _____

7. por fin / hombres / salir / corriendo del centro comercial

   _____

¿Te acuerdas?  Talking about the future   *Pupil's Edition, p. 305*

To talk about the future, you can use the present tense of **ir a** plus an infinitive: *Voy a comer* **con mis amigos esta tarde.** You can also use the simple future tense of the verb: *Comeré* **con mis amigos esta tarde.** The simple future tense is used less frequently than **ir a** + infinitive and is often considered more formal.

---

8 Help Adriana make her Career Day speech more formal by changing all the "**ir a**" constructions to the simple future. Underline each phrase first.

Hoy en día hay muchas posibilidades para los graduados. Por ejemplo, muchos de mis compañeros van a asistir a la universidad. Allí van a prepararse para carreras muy importantes. Algunos van a estudiar las ciencias, otros van a dedicarse a la ingeniería. Y otros van a ser médicos y enfermeros. Pero nosotros vamos a poder hacer más. Además de asistir a la universidad, también vamos a trabajar en nuestras comunidades.

1. _____   5. _____

2. _____   6. _____

3. _____   7. _____

4. _____

CAPÍTULO 12 Primer paso

98 Grammar and Vocabulary Workbook   ¡Ven conmigo! Level 3, Chapter 12

9 You're a script writer and the following dialogue script sounds a little too formal. Make the conversation more informal by changing the simple future tense to **ir a** + infinitive. Underline the verbs first.

ORIETA   Beatriz, ¿qué harás después de graduarte?

BEATRIZ   Bueno, asistiré a la universidad.

ORIETA   ¿Qué estudiarás en la universidad?

BEATRIZ   No sabré hasta que hable con mis padres. Ellos me aconsejarán algo.

ORIETA   ¿Qué crees que ellos te dirán?

BEATRIZ   Estoy segura que me sugerirán que estudie para ser doctora.

1. _____   5. _____

2. _____   6. _____

3. _____   7. _____

4. _____

10 You're putting together signs to warn people about what the world will be like if we don't change some of our habits. Use the future tense to complete each of the following sentences.

1. Hoy el aire está limpio, pero si manejamos nuestros coches demasiado, en 20 años... (estar)

_____

2. Hoy hay suficiente agua, pero si no la conservamos, en 20 años... (haber)

_____

3. Hoy tenemos bastante petróleo, pero si usamos demasiado, en 20 años... (tener)

_____

4. Hoy existen muchos animales, pero si destruimos las selvas tropicales, en 20 años... (morir)

_____

5. Hoy hay suficientes recursos, pero si no los conservamos, en 20 años... (acabársenos)

_____

11 Write a sentence using **ir a** + inf. to say what you think these people are going to do next.

1. Después de correr por 30 minutos, David...

_____

2. Después de estudiar por 2 horas, tú...

_____

3. Después de entrar en la biblioteca, Debra...

_____

4. Después de graduarse de la escuela secundaria, los estudiantes...

_____

5. Después de trabajar en el jardín todo el día, nosotros...

_____

CAPÍTULO 12 Primer paso

■ SEGUNDO PASO

In order to give advice about job interviews, you'll need to use the subjunctive with recommendations and after unknown or nonexistent antecedents. You'll also need to know appropriate vocabulary, as well as the conditional and the past subjunctive.

> ### *G*ramática de repaso   The subjunctive with recommendations   *Pupil's Edition, p. 310*
>
> After expressions like **es necesario que, recomendar que, sugerir que,** or any others that introduce suggestions or recommendations, use the subjunctive mood.
>
> **Recomiendo que estudies** para tu examen.
>
> **Sugiero que asistas** a la universidad si quieres superarte.

12 Mario is going on a few job interviews. Below are descriptions of each interviewer. Based on the description, write Mario a recommendation telling him how to behave. Use an appropriate phrase from the box.

no ser necesario	vestirse bien	recomendar	ser importante
sugerir	llegar a tiempo		
ponerse una corbata	aconsejar	ser espontáneo y sincero	prepararse

1. El señor Vargas es muy estricto y formal.

   _____
   _____

2. La señora Martínez es muy chistosa pero también sofisticada.

   _____
   _____

3. Al señor Dávila le gusta que uno esté bien preparado.

   _____
   _____

4. El señor Sifuentes es muy informal y es buena gente.

   _____
   _____

5. La señorita Suárez es muy amigable e informal.

   _____

13 Patricia is going on an interview tomorrow. Give her a suggestion based on the way she says she feels in each of the following sentences. Use the cues in parentheses.

    1. Estoy muy nerviosa. (sugerir / tomar las cosas con calma)

    _____

    2. No sé qué ponerme. (recomendar / vestirse bien)

    _____

    3. ¿A qué hora debo llegar? (ser importante / llegar a tiempo)

    _____

    4. Pienso salir con mis amigos la noche anterior. (aconsejar / acostarse temprano)

    _____

---

*G*ramática de repaso The subjunctive with the *Pupil's Edition, p. 311*
unknown or nonexistent

When referring back to someone or something nonexistent, unknown, or indefinite with **que**, use the subjunctive.

    No hay nada **que sea** interesante aquí.

    Busco una persona **que** me **pueda** ayudar.

---

14 Complete each sentence with either the present indicative or present subjunctive.

    1. Miguel trabaja para el periódico, donde no _____ (ganar) mucho dinero.

    2. Yo quiero un trabajo que _____ (pagar) más que el periódico.

    3. Mis padres conocen a un hombre que _____ (trabajar) para una empresa.

    4. He oído que esa empresa está buscando a alguien que _____ (hablar) inglés.

    5. También necesitan una persona que _____ (poder) trabajar por la tarde.

    6. Hasta ahora no han encontrado a nadie que _____ (cumplir) con estos requisitos.

15 Write employment ads for Compañía Cervantes, which needs to fill the following position at its local offices. Here are the jobs and their requirements.

    1. secretario / escribir a máquina

    _____

    2. técnico de computadoras / haber estudiado la ingeniería

    _____

    3. comerciante / haber terminado sus estudios secundarios

    _____

    4. contador / tener dos años de experiencia

    _____

CAPÍTULO 12 Segundo paso

16 Adela and Eduardo are shopping for a birthday present for Agustina. Read their conversation and fill in the blanks with either the present indicative or present subjunctive of the verb in parentheses.

ADELA   ¿Qué clase de regalo le **(1)** _____ (comprar) nosotros?

EDUARDO   Uno que no **(2)** _____ (ser) muy caro. ¿Qué tal esta blusa?

ADELA   Pero ¡qué fea es esa blusa! ¿Por qué no le compramos algo que ella

(3) _____ (poder) poner en la pared? Una pintura, por ejemplo.

EDUARDO   Buena idea, pero esta tienda no tendrá ninguna pintura que me

(4) _____ (gustar).

ADELA   Bueno, hay una tienda en el centro que **(5)** _____ (vender)

pinturas muy bonitas. Vamos allí.

EDUARDO   Ah, sí. Conozco esa tienda. Tengo un amigo que **(6)** _____

(trabajar) allí. Nos podrá vender una más barato.

VOCABULARIO   El mundo de los negocios   *Pupil's Edition, p. 312*

17 Gerardo wrote the following about his part time job. Read what he has to say. Then, using words from the box, complete the list with what Gerardo does and doesn't like about his job.

los empleados   el horario

la solicitud   los requisitos

el salario   los beneficios

el ambiente de trabajo

Me gusta el trabajo que tengo con Sociedad Comercial, S.A., aunque no creo que me paguen lo suficiente. Las horas que tengo que trabajar son buenas: trabajo por la tarde los martes y jueves y todo el día los sábados. La empresa también les ofrece tres días libres a todos los empleados y una semana de vacaciones. Por otro lado, no me gusta el lugar donde trabajo. Hay una sala donde los empleados pueden descansar pero es muy pequeña. Y las personas con quienes trabajo no son buena gente. Siempre están agobiadas y de mal humor.

Le gusta(n): _____

No le gusta(n): _____

18 Write the word that is being defined by each sentence. Use the vocabulary on page 312 of your textbook.

_____ 1. El papel que se llena cuando uno está buscando trabajo.

_____ 2. El papel que contiene una lista de todos los trabajos y toda la experiencia que una persona ha tenido.

_____ 3. Asegurar que todos los datos y toda la información son los más recientes.

_____ 4. La persona que supervisa a todos los empleados.

_____ 5. Las condiciones que uno tiene que cumplir para hacer un trabajo bien.

---

*G*ramática de repaso   The conditional and past   *Pupil's Edition, p. 313*
subjunctive

The past subjunctive after **si** expresses the hypothetical circumstances under which something would happen.

si yo quisier**a**	si nosotros quisiér**amos**
si tú quisier**as**	si vosotros quisiér**ais**
si él / ella / Ud. quisier**a**	si ellos / ella / Ud. quisier**an**

The conditional expresses what would happen under hypothetical circumstances.

yo solicitar**ía**	nosotros solicitar**íamos**
tú solicitar**ías**	vosotros solicitar**íais**
él / ella / Ud. solicitar**ía**	ellos / ellas / Uds. solicitar**ían**

---

19 Complete each of the following sentences with the past subjunctive and the conditional of the verbs in parentheses, as required by the context.

1. Si nosotros _____ (reciclar) toda nuestra basura, no

_____ (haber) tanta contaminación.

2. Si el gobierno _____ (realizar) unas campañas de educación,

_____ (eliminar) la drogadicción.

3. Si tú _____ (ser) bilingüe, _____ (poder)

encontrar un buen trabajo.

4. Si la gente no _____ (juzgar) tanto a otras personas, todos

_____ (llevarse) mejor.

CAPÍTULO 12 Segundo paso

20 Jeffrey is in the middle of an interview with Señora Calderón that isn't going too well. Using the cues, write sentences stating how the interview would be going if things were different.

1. si haber llegado a tiempo / señora Calderón no estar enojada

_____

_____

2. si llevar una corbata / sentirse más profesional

_____

_____

3. si tener su currículum vitae / poder mostrárselo a la señora Calderón

_____

_____

4. si no ser tan callado / la señora Calderón creer que es más confiado

_____

_____

5. si haberse acostado temprano / no tener sueño

_____

_____

6. si haber preparado unas preguntas / hacérselas a la señora Calderón

_____

_____

21 Each of the following sentences describes a problem that exists in the world today. For each situation, write a sentence stating how things would be if circumstances were different.

1. El aire está contaminado.

_____

_____

2. Se cometen muchos homicidios en las calles.

_____

_____

3. La gente prejuzga a personas diferentes.

_____

_____

4. Muchas parejas buscan un divorcio.

_____

_____